THE
NEW
FEDERALISM

The Hoover Institution
gratefully acknowledges generous support from

TAD TAUBE
TAUBE FAMILY FOUNDATION
KORET FOUNDATION

Founders of the Program on
American Institutions and Economic Performance

and Cornerstone gifts from

JOANNE AND JOHAN BLOKKER
SARAH SCAIFE FOUNDATION

THE
NEW
FEDERALISM

*Can the States
Be Trusted?*

Edited by
JOHN A. FEREJOHN
and
BARRY R. WEINGAST

Hoover Institution Press
Stanford University
Stanford, California

Hoover Institution Press Publication No. 443

Copyright © 1997 by the Board of Trustees of the
    Leland Stanford Junior University

First printing, 1997
03 02 01 00 99 98 97   9 8 7 6 5 4 3 2 1

Manufactured in the United States of America

The paper used in this publication meets the minimum requirements
of American National Standard for Information Sciences—Permanence
of Paper for Printed Library Materials, ANSI Z39.48–1984. ⊚

Library of Congress Cataloging-in-Publication Data

The new federalism : can the states be trusted? / edited by John Ferejohn
and Barry R. Weingast
        p.   cm.
    Includes bibliographical references and index.
    ISBN 0-8179-9512-9 (alk. paper)
    1. Federal government—United States.   2. State governments—
United States.   I. Ferejohn, John A.   II. Weingast, Barry R.
JK325.N47   1997
320.973—dc21   97-16799
                                                        CIP

CONTENTS

John A. Ferejohn and
Barry R. Weingast

INTRODUCTION

Can the States Be Trusted?

For the first 150 years of the American republic, the Supreme Court interpreted the Constitution as requiring strict limits on the national government's authority to regulate markets and promote public welfare. Consider the commerce clause, the national government's principal source of authority to regulate. Although a large part of modern America, the commerce clause went unused for nearly all the first hundred years of the Constitution. The federal government exercised this authority for the first time in 1887 with the inception of railroad regulation.

In the wake of the Great Depression, however, when Democrats sought to expand the national government under the New Deal, the Supreme Court dramatically weakened the constitutional limits on the federal government. Without these changes, the growth of the federal government in the 1960s and 1970s would not have been possible.

The growth of the federal government, increasingly the principal source of economic and social regulation, markedly altered American federalism. During America's first 150 years, economic regulation and the promotion of social welfare remained the domain of the states.[1] In the past sixty years, however, those powers have been shared, with the national government free to enter policy areas that had previously been the province of the states or that had not been subject to any government action.

Moreover, the national government's authority to enlist state governments in service of federal programs was greatly expanded through a broad judicial reading of the spending powers. For example, the Court permitted Congress to use federal money to induce state participation in Aid to Families with Dependent Children, food stamps, aid to education, and environmental policies. It also permitted Congress to tie federal funding of specific programs to the states' adopting unrelated federal policies. Thus Congress made receiving state highway funds contingent on the states' adopting the fifty-five-mile-an-hour speed limit and the minimum drinking age of twenty-one. The Court therefore allowed Congress to harness the ample administrative powers of state and local governments in service of national goals.

At the same time Congress was entering new policy domains, the courts were making use of their wider conception of federal commerce powers to invalidate various state actions. Many activities triggered judicial scrutiny that had previously been only distantly connected to interstate commerce. Court-imposed limitations combined with a more aggressive Congress to diminish the capacity of the states to act as autonomous governments within the federal system. No doubt this diminution of state authority shifted popular and journalistic attention away from the states to Washington, where the action was.

The expansive reading of Congress's enumerated powers could have been checked by the Tenth Amendment, which reserves those powers not delegated to Congress to the states or to the people. But, after a brief dalliance with this idea in the 1976 *National League of*

---

1. The courts did, however, place substantial restrictions on which regulations the states could actually promulgate.

Cities decision—which forbade Congress from regulating the wages and hours of municipal employees—a deeply divided Court abandoned this effort. In *Garcia* (1986), the Court asserted that the Tenth Amendment placed no limits on the expansion of congressional action.

In recent years, the growth of the federal government and its failure to resolve many major problems has raised questions about whether the national government is the appropriate regulator of all the problems it has taken on. Scholars and policymakers suggest that reinvigorating federalism may provide better solutions to many of the problems that the federal government has tackled unsuccessfully.

The reinvigoration of American federalism signals a dramatic departure from the recent past, forcing us to confront the question of whether it will yield better government. In this volume, we pose the question Can the states be trusted? and argue that there is no blanket answer.

For example, the long history of legal discrimination against African Americans demonstrates that states cannot be trusted on all dimensions of public policy. Competition among states is unlikely to prevent particular states from abrogating certain citizen rights—such as the right to vote and to public participation on an equal basis.

During the 1960s and 1970s, civil rights became the canonic case, as the national government took over one policy area after another, many of which had been the states' domain for more than a century. The public demand for solutions to perceived problems translated into intervention by the national government, for many people perceived that the problems they sought to address reflected state inaction or incapacity. Yet did the analogy from states' civil rights failures go too far? The widespread dissatisfaction with a mammoth federal bureaucracy, high taxes, and high costs of regulation suggests that it has.

If some took the civil rights analogy too far, proponents of small government use the mantle of federalism and especially states' rights to rationalize smaller government through a wholesale limiting of federal power. The purpose of this volume is to steer a middle ground.

We suggest that a range of policies is best assigned to the national government but, equally, that another range is best assigned to state and local governments. If the balance before the 1930s leaned too far toward the states, the balance since has tipped in the other direction. Hence, the purpose of this volume is to articulate a theoretical rationale for assigning policies to one government level instead of another and to suggest a range of policies, currently subject to federal regulation, that might be better served by giving power back to the states.

Although some politicians and interest groups support the new federalism merely because it promises to reduce government, this is not necessarily its effect. In fact, reassigning policy to lower levels of government will, under the right circumstances, produce more (state) government and better policy.

Recent Events

Events of the past few years promise significant changes in federalism, the most immediate of which are the changes associated with the Republican Congress since 1994, especially its Contract with America. During the past few years, congressional Republicans have proposed turning back major portions of federal authority to the states, introducing initiatives on, among other things, welfare, Medicaid, legal services, job training, and housing. These initiatives have thus far met with at least partial success.

Proponents of the new federalism hark back to an earlier era of states' rights and, to use Justice Louis Brandeis's famous phrase, the "laboratory of the states." Economists have long argued that jurisdictional competition under specific circumstances enhances public welfare, giving states the incentive to design cost-effective programs. Along with many state programs come multiple approaches to a particular problem—in contrast to a single national one. Multiple approaches in turn imply that states will imitate the most successful programs and that the less successful ones will be altered or dropped.[2] In sum, this view suggests that the new federalism will enhance public welfare.

Critics of the new federalism make the opposite argument: that turning power over to the states is tantamount to major reductions in programs. Those critics further argue that the Republicans' arguments about federalism, states' rights, and efficiency are a smoke screen for their ideological goal of cutting government. Competition among the · states, critics say, will not enhance efficiency but will force states to "race to the bottom" under pressure to maintain a low tax base and thus force lower levels of service.[3] In sum, this view suggests that the new federalism will lower public welfare.

In Washington the debate revolves primarily around ideology and position taking. Evidence and history frequently cannot make their way past the Washington beltway. Thus our project is designed to investigate the competing claims about the new federalism. Hence we ask, Can the states be trusted? and To what extent is there evidence favoring the competing claims on the new federalism?

This volume has three parts. In the first, the economists Ronald McKinnon and Tom Nechyba survey the literature providing the theory and evidence on federalism. Part two contains three investigations of competition among the states in the areas of welfare policy, environment policy, and corporate chartering. Part three concludes the volume with a general discussion of the political parameters of federalism.

---

2. Two important studies by economists are Timothy Besley and Anne Case, "Incumbent Behavior: Vote-Seeking, Tax-Setting, and Yardstick Competition," *American Economic Review* 85 (1995): 24–45, and Caroline Minter Hoxby, "Are Efficiency and Equity in School Finance Substitutes or Complements?" *Journal of Economic Perspectives* 10 (fall 1996): 51–72.

3. See, for example, Paul E. Peterson and Mark C. Rom, *Welfare Magnets: A New Case for a National Standard* (Washington, D.C.: Brookings Institution, 1990).

Summary of the Papers

McKinnon and Nechyba survey the principal economic lessons concerning federalism. They proceed in two parts: first they ask under what conditions is federalism desirable and, second, how can such a system best be financed? To address these questions, they turn to the economic arguments about how government services are best provided within the context of a federal system.

Economists conclude that deciding on the best jurisdiction to provide a particular service depends on the characteristics of that service. If a given amount of the service can be provided more cheaply when it is produced for many rather than few citizens (national defense), if the benefits of the service extend over a large geographic area (certain types of pollution control), or if decentralization would lead to "bad" competition among the states or inequitable outcomes across states, these services should be provided by the national government. If, in contrast, local tastes for a particular government activity differ widely (spending on recreational facilities), if localized information needs to be taken into account to provide the service most effectively (schools), or if competition between local governments leads to healthy competition and innovative local policy experiments, state and local governments are better suited to provide the service.

McKinnon and Nechyba raise important issues about how to finance state and local government. Standard arguments in the economics literature suggest that revenue should be raised at the central level and then handed down to lower governments. McKinnon and Nechyba challenge this conclusion, arguing that it ignores the political implications and that having the national government provide revenue to state and local governments breaks the link between local prosperity and local decision making. McKinnon and Nechyba do not argue against the provision of funds by the national to lower governments; instead, they show that problems arise when the federal government bails out states in financial distress, diminishing the efficacy of competition among the states.

To illustrate this principle, they compare the recovery of the American South in the last three decades, long one of the poorest regions of the United States, with the highly subsidized Maritime provinces in Canada and southern Italy's Mezzogiorno region. McKinnon and Nechyba argue that the huge subsidies to the Maritimes and the Mezzogiorno provide no incentive for these regions to develop. In contrast, the recovery of the American South reflects local incentives providing a healthier economic base. McKinnon and Nechyba argue that, had the South been highly subsidized, it would not have recovered.[4]

Craig Volden provides the first empirical study, focusing on the critical area of welfare, specifically, Aid to Families with Dependent Children (AFDC). Congress recently passed legislation granting states greater discretion over welfare policy. Critics of the legislation appeal to the race to the bottom argument: competition will force states to lower benefit levels in order to lower taxes. Volden suggests three reasons why this will not happen. First, existing federal legislation has long granted states the freedom to set certain aspects of benefit levels, implying that, were there a race to the bottom, it would have already occurred. Second, pressure by compassionate populations and the bureaucrats running welfare programs weigh against such reductions. Finally, Volden reports that the evidence suggests that states rarely cut welfare spending in areas where they have freedom to set benefit levels. Only in a fraction of cases has there been a cut of 10 percent or more, and most of these cuts were later reversed. Historically, the biggest source of benefit reduction, Volden argues, has not been state competition but national inflation.

Richard Revesz studies state competition in the area of environ-

---

4. See Ronald McKinnon, "Market-Preserving Federalism in the American Monetary Union," in Mario Blejer and Teresa Ter-Minassian, eds., *Macroeconomic Dimensions of Public Finance: Essays in Honor of Vito Tanzi* (London: Routledge 1997).

mental regulation. He reports that scholars and policymakers tend to prefer federal over state regulation of the environment, first, because state regulation would lead to a race to the bottom as states compete for capital and firms by relaxing regulatory standards so as to lower costs to firms wishing to locate within their borders. The second concerns a type of externality: pollution that crosses state borders. Both reasons, it is alleged, require federal intervention.

Revesz turns these issues on their head. With respect to the externality argument, he shows that current national environmental laws are either ineffective or, worse, counterproductive. With respect to the race to the bottom, he argues that the evidence points in the opposite direction: interstate competition does not lead to the bottom.

Roberta Romano provides our third empirical study, investigating state competition for corporate charters. She suggests that the codes defining corporate charters promote economic welfare by maximizing shareholder value. In other words, federalism and competition among the states work satisfactorily. Evaluating William Cary's claim that there is race to the bottom in the provisions governing incorporation, she argues that firms are located in markets, not states. States with inferior codes impose higher costs of capital, thereby putting firms chartered in those states at a competitive disadvantage. As a consequence, firms are likely to seek charters in states that lower their costs of capital and hence give them a competitive edge. This in turn provides the incentive for states to provide efficacious codes. Romano summarizes considerable evidence from the literature supporting her claims.

Part three concludes our volume. There we raise a set of deep political concerns about the relative merits of a statutory versus a constitutional basis for the new federalism.

PART ONE

Ronald McKinnon and
Thomas Nechyba

CHAPTER ONE | # Competition in Federal Systems
The Role of Political and Financial Constraints

Introduction

The purpose of this chapter is to evaluate the current public finance literature on federalism critically and to use the evidence to come to a conclusion regarding what we have learned thus far. Although there are substantial economic arguments suggesting that federal systems, if appropriately structured, achieve outcomes superior to unitary governments, both externality and equity concerns suggest a strong role for central government direction of lower tiers through systems of grants and mandates. The case for such federal involvement in state and local affairs as well as in community affairs, however, weakens considerably once political constraints on government behavior are taken into account; the case for national grants is further weakened once the role of monetary and financial constraints is considered. We therefore conclude that the strengths of a federal system are best brought forth when tax bases and government responsibilities are carefully (and constitutionally) assigned to different tiers (including the assignment of monetary policy to the central level) but where annually legislated fiscal interactions between different tiers are strictly limited.

In the second section we begin our argument by highlighting the traditional *public finance* principles relevant to the discussion of federalism. These principles relate to *nonmonetary* economic forces within federations and do not consider the role of political institutions. The third section introduces the complication brought about by politics, and the fourth section raises additional complications due to the impact of monetary institutions in competitive environments. The final section draws some basic policy conclusions based on the findings in the previous sections of the chapter.

The Public Finance Literature on Fiscal Federalism

Federalism is not a new topic to economics in general or to public finance in particular. Since the defining contribution of Musgrave (1959), who laid out some broad guidelines regarding the optimal division of responsibilities in a federal system, public finance economists (see, for example, papers in Oates [1991]) have developed basic notions of efficiency and equity that guide the economist's thinking on federalism. More precisely, in the public finance literature that we consider in this section, researchers attempt to isolate the various economic forces at work within federalist systems by modeling different levels of governments as benevolent institutions whose sole objective is to maximize the "public's welfare" *within* its jurisdiction.[1] This assumption represents neither a positive judgment nor an ideological statement regarding the economist's view of how real-world governments behave but rather is part of a deliberate attempt to assume away the complexities of politics in order to focus solely on economic forces. (We will relax this assumption in the third section.)

---

1. Some approaches assume that governments maximize a social welfare function; others assume that each government maximizes the welfare of a representative resident.

Within this context, three broad topics have been analyzed: (1) the optimal assignment of *government services* (expenditures and regulation) to different tiers of government, (2) the optimal assignment of *tax bases*, and (3) the optimal kind and level of *fiscal interaction* between the various tiers. Without attempting an exhaustive review of the entire literature, we discuss in this section the basic economic principles that emerge in each of these three areas.

GOVERNMENT SERVICES:
THE ECONOMIC ARGUMENT FOR FEDERALISM

Federalism is, in essence, a compromise between two extreme forms of government: a fully centralized unitary government on the one hand and a fully decentralized system of many states or localities on the other. It is therefore natural to begin by asking the most basic question: Why are we interested in such a compromise in the first place? We argue here that the *public finance* argument for a multi-tiered system arises from the very different characteristics of the services provided by the government sector. Each of these characteristics makes provision of a specific service either more or less amenable to central provision. Thus, the characteristics of government services give rise to both centralizing and decentralizing economic forces that combine to define the appropriate level of government that ought to provide each type of service.

The Need for a Central Government—Centralizing Forces

We begin with the characteristics of government services that act as centralizing forces. These can generally be classified into two major categories: *externalities* and a desire for *equity*. The first of these (externalities) arises in three distinct ways: (1) the *nonrivalrous* nature of "national" public goods imparts significant cost advantages to centralized provision of certain goods (national defense); (2) the *spatial non-*

excludability of some public activities gives rise to positive geographic spillovers that cause lower-tier governments to underprovide these goods (environmental protection); and (3) the *mobility* of certain factors creates incentives for local governments to generate externalities purposefully by attempting to "export" social problems to other localities or to "import" desirable features. The second major force for centralization (equity concerns) is more philosophically and ideologically rooted and depends on the definition of equity used in policy analysis. We begin with a discussion of externality effects and then briefly discuss the role of equity.

An externality occurs whenever the actions of one entity directly affect another entity. When a government provides national defense, for example, this action affects directly (and positively) all citizens of the country that is being protected. Goods that represent such positive externalities are called *public goods,* and their essential feature is that the consumption of the good is *nonrivalrous*—one person's consumption (of the protection provided by national defense) does not take away from another person's consumption of the same good. Some public goods are national in scope in that their benefits are felt equally by all residents without regard to geographic location (national public goods), whereas others are local in the sense that the benefit derived from these goods declines with geographic distance from the place where the good is produced. The nuclear missiles kept in silos in California, for example, provide a deterrent to foreign attacks regardless of whether a citizen resides in Los Angeles or New York. Central Park in New York City, in contrast, may be of great benefit to residents of Manhattan but of little use to residents of Los Angeles, and the Fourth of July fireworks display in Los Angeles is of little consequence to New York residents.

Economic theory suggests that the appropriate level of government to provide a given public good critically depends on the degree of spatial nonrivalry of that good. Imagine, for example, the (admittedly absurd) proposition that school districts should provide their own nuclear deterrents against external threats. This would require substantial duplication of investment in nuclear arsenals when the same objective could be met at a significantly lower (per person) cost by the central government (since the same nuclear arsenal can protect both Los Angeles and New York). The *national nonrivalry embodied in national public goods thus gives rise to large cost advantages to central governments* whose constituents are numerous because the total expense of providing the good is independent of the size of the population. Similar cost advantages arise when, for example, effective regulation requires substantial investment in specialized expertise that is more efficiently done at the central level rather than by fifty different state governments. At the same time, there is no such cost advantage to having the central government provide such goods as local neighborhood parks because the nonrivalry of these goods only extends over a small geographic area.

A second type of externality arises when the benefits of a public good are enjoyed by both residents and nonresidents living outside the political jurisdiction providing the good. Since the local government in these circumstances is unable to limit the benefits to local residents, we will call the class of such public goods and services *spatially nonexcludable*. Environmental regulations restricting the emissions of greenhouse gases may, for example, protect people (almost) equally regardless of where they reside. Thus, when lower-tier governments are assigned the responsibility of setting such environmental policies, these policies have inherent positive *spillovers* in the sense that residents outside the local jurisdiction benefit as much from the reduction in greenhouse gases as do people within the jurisdiction. Since each political entity maximizes the welfare of only the citizens *within* that entity, a local jurisdiction underestimates the total (social) benefit of additional reductions in greenhouse gas emissions and thus provides too little environmental protection. Similarly, macroeconomic stabilization policies, if conducted at the state rather than the federal level, would have inherent spillover effects on other states.[2] Centralization of such activities eliminates these spillover problems because the central government takes into account the welfare of all its citizens, not just those residing in one locality or state (Oates 1972).[3]

Finally, a third type of externality arises when *mobility* (of certain crucial factors) provides incentives to lower-tier governments to export particular local problems or to import local benefits from other districts. Unlike the other two types of externalities, which are inherent in the nature of certain government activities, this third type is *intentionally created* by lower-tier governments when certain responsibilities are assigned to them.[4] In the recent welfare debate, for example, some argued that assigning responsibility over welfare policy to state governments will lead to a "race to the bottom" as each state attempts to export the problem of poverty by setting welfare benefits so low that the poor will migrate to high-benefit states.[5] Similarly, it has been argued that

---

2. Although public finance economists have generally agreed that stabilization policies are therefore most appropriately handled by the central government, Gramlich (1987) argues that standard arguments regarding spillover effects of state macroeconomic policies are overstated as macroeconomic problems are increasingly more regional and as mobility of factors and labor across state lines is costly.

3. The second externality differs from the first in that it arises from the nonexcludability rather than the nonrivalry of public goods. More precisely, although it is feasible for each state to provide its own defense from outsiders without affecting the level of protection enjoyed by another state (unless the two are bound by treaties), it is *not* feasible for states to restrict the benefits from decreased greenhouse gas emissions to their political boundaries. Therefore, *nonrivalry implies that any given amount of a public good can be produced more cheaply (per capita) at the central level, and nonexcludability implies that the center will choose a more efficient level of the good than the lower tiers.*

4. Starrett (1980) and Gordon (1983) formally define the various sources of such externalities to include congestion effects outside the locality, changes in tax revenues in other communities because of various spillovers, and price distortions in other communities due to one community's policies.

5. Craig Volden analyzes welfare policy in a chapter in this volume, and Epple and

states may attempt to import desirable high-income residents and firms by lowering welfare payments (and thus lowering the amount of redistribution within the state). Since whenever one jurisdiction successfully exports its problems, another must import those same problems, the only result from such competition is a distortion of policies away from what is optimal. Such distortions could be avoided by a central government that takes into account costs and benefits for all residents.[6]

Quite apart from the efficiency arguments for centralization that arise out of the three types of externalities above, a further consideration involves particular notions of equity. Suppose, for example, that equity in the provision of public schools was defined as equality of spending (as it was by the California Supreme Court for public school spending in the later versions of *Serrano vs Priest*). Since there is little hope that an unhampered decentralized system would achieve this equity standard, some have argued that it requires the centralization of education finance (as has happened in California). Thus, an equality of outcomes standard of equity in the provision of a particular service naturally leads to centralization of that service. Other equity standards, however, may lead to different conclusions. An equality of opportunity standard, for example, would recognize that different populations may require different types and amounts of spending on public education and would demand a system in which each locality, given similar "ef-

---

Romer (1991) suggest that redistribution at the lower-tier level may be quite prevalent even in the presence of substantial mobility.

6. Besharov and Zweiman (1997) recently introduced the idea of a different type of spillover that arises out of increasing returns to scale and differential sizes of jurisdictions. For example, for much of the history of car emissions regulations, California has imposed stiffer regulations than other states. Since California is a large market, car makers, rather than produce separately for California, often simply adopt the California standards nationally. Large states may therefore be able to export their policies to other states. To what extent such potential spillovers introduce an additional centralizing or decentralizing force remains uncertain and relatively unexplored.

forts," would be able to meet its needs. Advocates of this standard often argue for intergovernmental grants that equalize opportunities across school districts. We will discuss this further.

The Need for Local Governments — Decentralizing Forces

Having outlined the basic economic forces leading to more efficient (and equitable) provision of public services at a central level, we can proceed to ask whether, within the economic model of benevolent governments at each tier, there in fact is *any* gain from providing some types of services in a more decentralized way. In particular, consider public services that are subject to none of the externality forces discussed above, and suppose, for now, that there were no equity considerations. If decentralization of those services led to a desirable outcome, would it not be possible for the central government to simply mimic the decentralized government behavior?

The answer is a qualified yes. *If* (1) tastes were identical for the entire population, *if* (2) knowledge concerning tastes and local conditions were readily available to the benevolent central government, and *if* (3) government planners could accurately predict all policy consequences, the central government would be in a position to replicate the federalist outcome precisely. When a country's population is relatively homogeneous (as, for example, in Sweden), the first condition may be satisfied and the latter two conditions may seem reasonable. In the United States, however, condition (1) clearly does not hold as the population is enormously diverse in both its tastes and its needs. Given this large diversity, the informational requirements embodied in conditions (2) and (3) are equivalent to assuming a kind of omniscience on the part of the central government that is unlikely to hold true. As Hayek (1945) taught long ago, to assume such omniscience "is to assume the problem away and to disregard everything that is important and significant in the real world."[7] Thus, a large part of the problem of designing optimal governing institutions, especially in societies as diverse as that of the United States, involves constructing these institutions in such a way that they not only legislate good public policies but also extract the knowledge and information necessary for determining the nature of such policies. The incorporation of lower-tier governments into a federal system provides a potentially powerful means by which this can be accomplished in at least three distinct ways: (1) the existence of such governments encourages the emergence of geographically concentrated homogeneous subpopulations despite a heterogeneous national population; (2) given the closer proximity to their constituents, local governments face lower informational barriers in discovering local tastes and needs; and (3) in the absence of perfect information regarding policy consequences, lower-tier governments can serve as relatively low-cost laboratories for policy experiments and thus generate additional information regarding which kinds of public policies may have positive outcomes.

The first of these effects has been well known since the seminal contribution of Tiebout (1956), who suggested that the existence of many competing governments may create forces analogous to market forces in that households and individuals can self-select into political jurisdictions that pursue policies most closely matched with their tastes. In the same way as different types of individuals choose different shopping centers that provide varying mixes of products and services,

---

7. In fact, if we were comfortable with this assumption, we could dispense with all forms of decentralization (Hayek 1945). Just as a government could calculate the federalist outcome, it could calculate the proper allocation of eggs and butter without relying on the information arising from a decentralized price system. A key economic justification for decentralization of government services is thus related to the argument for decentralized provision of private goods. This should not be surprising; restricting a particular activity solely to voluntary private exchange is, after all, an extreme form of decentralization to the smallest level of government (the family and the individual).

under decentralization these individuals will choose (by deciding where to live) different types of communities that provide varying mixes of public services. To the extent that individuals take local policies into account in their residential location choices, migration forces thus create multiple lower-tier political jurisdictions that exhibit heterogeneity in tastes *across* jurisdictions but homogeneity of tastes *within* them.[8] This enables lower-tier governments to tailor policies to specific local tastes and needs, while facilitating a process by which these tastes and needs are more easily identified.

Second, it is likely that, even if a completely centralized government were able to replicate the Tiebout distribution of geographically concentrated tastes, local government officials have inherently better information concerning local conditions and local preferences. In the United States, for example, public schools have traditionally been viewed as a responsibility of local governments because of the localized needs of different types of children (local information) and the localized tastes of parents who demand different types of schools in different communities (local tastes). Thus, the federal government (or even a state government) is likely to have insufficient information to tailor neighborhood schools to local needs and tastes and would tend to provide a one-size-fits-all school system that may not meet individual local demands. (Again, this is clearly less of a factor in more-homogeneous societies where public education could more easily be provided by the center.) So long as there are no strong externality or equity arguments in favor of centralization, local provision therefore has in-

---

8. The U.S. population is remarkably mobile. About 20 percent of the U.S. population moves annually (U.S. Dept. of Commerce 1991). For empirical support of the importance of local public services in these moves, see Oates (1969), Gramlich and Rubinfeld (1982), Nechyba and Strauss (1997), and references therein. Furthermore, Scotchmer (1994) provides a summary of the extensive theoretical Tiebout literature, and Nechyba (1997a) reviews the available positive models. Rubinfeld (1978) provides a comprehensive treatment of a variety of issues in the Tiebout setting.

herent advantages not accessible to less-informed central governments.[9]

Finally, sometimes the economic impact of policy initiatives is uncertain because of lack of experience and the inability of governments to predict changes in individual behavior resulting from a proposed policy shift. In 1994, for example, although the U.S. population seemed interested in reforming the health care system, it was hesitant to launch a large national experiment in the face of little information regarding the consequences of such an untried system. Therefore, the national plan was rejected in favor of continuing to have states act as "laboratories of experiments." These experiments may be more successful because of additional local information and, even in the absence of such informational advantages, may *generate information* that was previously unavailable.

We have thus identified the characteristics of government services that lead to more-efficient provision of those services at either the central or a lower-tier level of government in the absence of political and monetary distortions. These characteristics, and their implication for the public finance debate on federalism, are summarized in table 1. In many cases there is, of course, legitimate debate among policymakers regarding the relative strengths of the centralizing and decentralizing characteristics of a particular service. Ultimately, this debate cannot be resolved without the type of empirical analysis that the other chapters in this book offer.

---

9. Spillover effects from local public education may materialize because, for example, a better educated population makes better electoral choices and commits fewer crimes. Empirical evidence, however, indicates that most of the benefits from public education accrue directly to local residents (Wyckoff 1996). Much of the debate regarding the merits of centralizing public education therefore deals with equity rather than efficiency concerns, and Hoxby (1995) provides evidence that equity-motivated centralization results in decreases in educational attainments (efficiency).

Table 1   Assignment of Responsibilities to Different Tiers:
An Economic Case for Federalism

Centralizing Forces	*Externalities*		
	Nonrivalry of national public goods	→ Cost advantages from centralization	Nuclear deterrents Investments in specialized expertise and training
	Nonexcludability of public goods	→ Lower tiers generate positive spillovers, provide too little	Environmental protection Macrostabilization
	Mobility-induced externalities	→ Lower tiers distort policies to export weaknesses and import strengths	"Race to the bottom" Zoning for high-smokestack industries
	Equity Equality of outcomes	→ Equity standard that urges uniformity of public goods	Equal protection clause (as interpreted by the California Supreme Court for public education)
Decentralizing Forces	*Diversity of Tastes*	→ "Voting with feet" results in locally homogeneous tastes	Average tastes in Louisiana differ from those in New York
	Lack of Information Local tastes and needs	→ Local information may be less costly to access by lower tier	Public schools Neighborhood amenities
	Uncertainty over the impact of new policies	→ New information is generated via local policy experiments	Health care reform

TAXATION IN A FEDERAL SYSTEM:
CONDITIONS FOR EFFICIENT LOWER-TIER COMPETITION

Given that a federal system with an appropriate assignment of government expenditure responsibilities is potentially more efficient than a system of unitary government(s), the next natural question that arises is, How should each tier in such a system be financed? In particular, we begin in this section by asking which tax instruments ought to be assigned to which tier of government and then proceed in the next section to ask whether additional gains can be achieved from intergovernmental transfers.

Much of the literature on optimal tax assignments relies on intuitions similar to those we developed in the previous section. In particular, just as each lower-tier government ignores the consequences of its expenditure and regulatory policies on nonresidents, it also ignores the consequences of its tax policy on other localities. If local tax policy has spillover effects, it therefore will not result in an optimal use of that policy when left to the local government. Furthermore, lower-tier governments are sometimes able to use their tax policies intentionally to generate externalities that benefit the residents within that political jurisdiction but cause net social harm when all citizens of the federation are considered. Potential spillover distortions of lower-tier taxation fall into three major categories: (1) *tax exporting*; (2) *unhealthy tax competition* owing to the mobility of some tax bases; and (3) the under- or over*taxation of activities that themselves have spillover effects*.

The first of these distortions arises from the ability of communities to export certain types of taxes. Consider, for example, the state of Florida. With its vast tourism industry, the state relies heavily on sales taxes, which are paid in great part by nonresidents (who do not consume many services) and are thus exported outside the state. Tourists are thus subsidizing government spending in Florida through their contribution to the state treasury and are thus providing incentives for the state government (which considers only the welfare of Floridians) to overuse the sales tax. In assigning tax bases optimally within a federal system, economic theory therefore suggests that, all else being equal, lower-tier governments ought to be restricted to the use of taxes that are not easily exported.

For this purpose, we can draw a useful distinction between two types of taxes: *resident-based taxes*, which tax factors of production (like labor, land, and capital) based on the owner's residence and tax goods and services based on the residence of the consumer; and *source-based taxes*, which tax factors where they are employed and goods and services where they are consumed. Thus, if a state requires all residents to register their cars with the State Department of Motor Vehicles, and if it taxes all registered vehicles (as many states do), this is a resident-based tax because the only consumers liable for the tax are those who reside within the state and own automobiles (regardless of where the automobiles were purchased). If, however, the state imposes a sales tax on all cars purchased within the state, this is a source-based tax because a consumer is liable for the tax regardless of whether he is a resident of the state.[10] The crucial difference between these types of taxes is that source-based taxes can often be exported, whereas resident-based taxes cannot.[11] Our conclusion thus far therefore implies that *lower-tier gov-*

---

10. Similarly, a wage tax that is charged by a municipality to all workers who earn wages in that municipality is a source-based tax on labor, whereas a wage tax charged to all residents of a municipality regardless of where these wages were earned would be a residence-based tax on labor. A sales tax in Florida can be converted into a purely resident-based tax if out-of-state residents can claim a refund for the sales taxes they pay in Florida.

11. Consumption taxes can be exported whenever a good is scarce outside a jurisdiction (as, for example, Disney World) and consumers are thus forced to purchase that good in a particular location. Exporting of factor taxes, in contrast, can occur whenever a factor is relatively immobile (like land) and is used in the production of an export commodity. Given the relatively high mobility of most factors (in particular, labor and capital; see Grieson [1980], Feldstein and Vaillant [1994], Papke [1991], and Feldstein [1994]), lower-tier governments are limited in their ability to export taxes on these factors. Similar types of issues arise when localities tax exports that are produced by non-competitive industries. See also Arnott and Grieson (1981), McLure and Mieszkowski

ernments should, whenever possible, *be restricted to resident-based taxes to avoid tax exporting.*

There are, however, two potential qualifications to this traditional argument against tax exporting relying on residence-based taxes. First, people who are not permanent residents but are nevertheless taxed within the jurisdiction (e.g., tourists in Florida paying the state sales tax) may impose substantial local costs on the jurisdiction in the form of police and fire protection as well as other public facilities. To the extent that tax revenues from nonresidents pay for services directly enjoyed by those nonresidents, tax exporting does not occur. Second, McKinnon (1997) suggests that a uniform states sales tax may be a natural outcome of benign horizontal tax competition among middle-level governments with "hard" budget constraints and that differenti-ated taxes are difficult to sustain in such an environment. If such com-petition across governments leads to a more compititve provision of goods and services, the scope for any one middle-level government exercising sufficient monopoly power in one good or service to be able to shift taxes to nonresidents is limited.

A second potential distortion arises from the *mobility* of tax bases. Consider, for example, taxes on capital. To the extent that capital is mobile within a federation, lower-tier governments will tend to keep such taxes low to prevent capital from fleeing the local political juris-diction. What the locality does not consider, however, is that, whenever capital moves out of the local jurisdiction, it moves into another juris-diction, thereby making revenue collection easier elsewhere. Again the potential inefficiency arises because the lower-tier government consid-ers only the impact of its policies on local residents.[12] To the extent

---

(1983), and Mintz and Tulkens (1996) for various applications; see Pindyck (1978) and Kolstad and Wolak (1983, 1985) for empirical illustrations.

12. For a more detailed analysis of tax competition for capital, see Mieszkowski (1972), Wilson (1986), Zodrow and Mieszkowski (1986), Wildasin (1989), Gordon (1992). A conceptually slightly different but related effect arises from tax competition when local governments seek to attract local income-enhancing activities (like certain

that a tax base is mobile, it will therefore be underutilized by lower-tier governments. This leads to our second conclusion: all else being equal, *lower-tier governments ought to be assigned tax bases that are relatively immobile.*[13]

Finally, additional distortions may enter whenever localities are permitted to tax activities that themselves give rise to geographic spill-overs that extend beyond local boundaries. For example, if localities are given the power to tax an activity (landfills) whose costs are local-ized and whose benefits are spread out (beyond the community bound-ary), then, whenever the activity is a net loss to the community, the community will overtax it in an attempt to curtail it.[14] Similarly, when-ever a community is allowed to tax an activity that has localized bene-fits and geographically diffuse costs, the community will tend to under-tax (or subsidize) the activity. An example may be high-smokestack industries. Because of the height of the smokestacks, such industries spread pollution well beyond local boundaries. Local communities may therefore seek to attract such industries with low taxes because their residents are not affected by the pollution that is being generated.

The various potential distortions in local tax policies are summa-

---

industries) without considering that this reduces incomes elsewhere. This is known as a "beggar-thy-neighbor" policy (Inman and Rubinfeld 1996) and often results in inef-ficient subsidies (Oates & Schwab 1988).

13. Tax competition is empirically not relevant for most consumption taxes unless jurisdictions are small and cross-border shopping is large, but it is relevant to taxation of mobile factors like labor and capital (see Kimbell and Harrison [1984], Jones and Whalley [1988], Morgan, Mutti, and Partridge [1989], and Wildasin [1986, 1997]). Of course, to the extent to which taxes on mobile factors (like capital) are used to provide services directly benefiting those factors, these taxes induce no factor mobility and the tax externality does not occur.

14. This distortion is known as the "not-in-my-backyard" (NIMBY) effect and typi-cally results in prohibitive taxation of certain types of activities (like landfills) (Inman and Rubinfeld 1996). As mentioned later, it can also arise more generally under equal-izing grants that discourage local tax base formation (see, for example, Hoxby [1997]).

rized in table 2. The basic principles emerging from this table can be summarized as follows: lower-tier governments should be limited to predominantly resident-based taxation (to prevent tax exporting) and to tax bases that are relatively immobile (to prevent unhealthy tax competition). Furthermore, they should be limited in their taxing authority over activities that generate significant spatial externalities.[15]

CENTRAL GOVERNMENT INTERVENTION AND EFFICIENCY

Although a strong economic argument for federalism based on the tension between the centralizing and decentralizing forces discussed earlier can clearly be made, it is by now equally clear that there are too many potential economic distortions on both the tax and the spending sides for us to expect a federalist system to be perfectly optimal (even when all assignments have been made appropriately and when all governments are assumed to be interested solely in maximizing their constituents' welfare). It has therefore been suggested (Oates [1972], Rivlin [1992]) that when substantial local informational advantages and diversity of local tastes call for decentralization of a particular public service, the central government can play an additional positive role whenever there are remaining externality or equity problems associated with decentralization. In particular, although local provision gives rise to the benefits of decentralization, the national government can introduce into this system the benefits of centralization by designing incentives for local governments to behave more optimally. Such incentives can be created through the use of (1) intergovernmental grants and (2) central government mandates.

---

15. An alternative to assigning taxes is to pursue "tax harmonization," which eliminates lower-tier discretion over tax rates. As this is more relevant to the European Union, we forgo a discussion of it here. See Inman and Rubinfeld (1996) for a brief discussion, and see Frey and Eichenberg (1996) for a public choice perspective.

Table 2   Potential Lower-Tier Tax Externalities

Tax Exporting	Source-based taxes	→ The ability to export the tax causes lower-tier overuse of that tax	Consumption taxes of locally concentrated goods (tourism) Taxation of immobile factors
Tax Competition	Mobile tax bases	→ Taxes are underutilized by lower tier	Taxation of mobile factors Sales taxes in small districts
	"Beggar-thy-neighbor" policies	→ Lower tiers bid for desirable industries	Subsidies for Mercedes plants Tax abatements for sports teams
Taxation of Activities with Spillovers	Taxes on activities with concentrated local costs and diffuse benefits	→ Lower tier taxes the activity too heavily (NIMBY)	Taxation of landfills
	Taxes on activities with diffuse costs and concentrated benefits	→ Lower tier taxes the activity too little (or subsidizes it)	Taxation of high-smokestack industries

The current welfare reform serves as an instructive example. Over the past several decades, many welfare programs (in particular Aid to Families with Dependent Children [AFDC]) were administered by state governments (under federal guidelines and restrictions), and benefit levels were set by the states. Because of the fear that state competition would lead to an underfunding of such benefits (as states attempt to export the poor by setting benefit levels low and import the rich by limiting redistributive taxation), the federal government created a matching-grant system; for every dollar spent on AFDC within a state, the federal government contributed at least one additional dollar to the state AFDC program. Thus each dollar of additional spending on AFDC cost state taxpayers only fifty cents (or less in many cases). The fear that states would underfund AFDC was therefore countered by federal incentives that lowered the price of spending on AFDC faced by states.[16]

More recently, as the AFDC program was reformed into the Temporary Assistance to Needy Families (TANF) program, the federal government changed incentives faced by states. The policy reform was motivated by a widespread feeling that the AFDC program was too centralized in terms of the restrictions it placed on state welfare policies; the TANF program now places considerably fewer such restrictions on states. At the same time, the fiscal incentives faced by state governments changed dramatically. Whereas the federal contribution to the AFDC program was in the form of *matching* grants, the federal contribution to the TANF program is in the form of *block* grants, which give states a lump sum amount that is independent of the state's own spending on welfare. Thus, whereas an additional dollar of state welfare spending under AFDC cost the state fifty cents (or less, depending on the federal matching rate), an additional dollar of spending (beyond the level of the block grant) on welfare under TANF now costs the states precisely one dollar. Given the potential strength of the price effect contained in matching grants, state spending on welfare would therefore be expected to decline as we switch to a system of block grants. To alleviate such concerns, the TANF legislation contained an additional mandate that requires states to spend a minimum fraction of what they previously spent on AFDC.

The AFDC and TANF programs therefore illustrate two alternative ways in which central involvement in the fiscal affairs of lower-tier governments can change lower-tier policy. Under the former system, the federal government used *price incentives* to encourage states to spend more on AFDC; under the new system the federal government mandates a certain minimum spending level (and contributes a lump sum amount to that level) but leaves the price faced by states undis-

---

16. Such price incentives tend to be effective in changing state government behavior (Moffitt 1984).

torted. Without such mandates, economic theory predicts that block grants would have relatively little impact on state incentives unless they were very large. In particular, if the total block grant to the lower-tier government is smaller than what that government would have chosen to spend on the program without any grants, then the lower tier can simply shift the resources it would have devoted to the program to other purposes (spending programs or tax cuts). Such block grants are therefore theoretically equivalent to simple cash infusions, and they contain no real incentives for states to spend additional resources on specific programs (beyond what they would have spent on their own).[17]

The different types of efficiency or equity-enhancing central government interventions are summarized in table 3. First, central governments can use mandates to control lower-tier policies. Such mandates may include tax base assignments to lower-tier governments that are made in accordance with the criteria laid out in the previous section, as well as minimum or maximum spending (or regulatory) mandates in certain areas (such as the minimum spending requirement under TANF). Second, the center may use several types of grants to lower-tier governments. If positive spillovers or mobility-induced competition cause an underprovision of a specific decentralized government activity, then matching grants that change the relative price of providing more of that activity can be structured in such a way as to "internalize" the externalities that cause the inefficiencies.[18] Furthermore, similar

---

17. For a theoretical illustration of different types of grants, see Oates (1972); for an early empirical analysis, see Strauss (1974); and for more general simulations, see Nechyba (1996). Hoxby (1997) offers a recent empirical analysis of state grants, and Craig and Inman (1985) demonstrate empirically how states use federal grants to increase spending in other budget categories as well as to cut taxes.

18. Similarly, if tax exporting causes lower-tier governments to overuse certain tax instruments, negative central government matching aid would be appropriate (Boadway and Flatters 1982). Furthermore, equity and efficiency objectives could also be met by central government grants directed at *local voters* rather than *local governments*. In particular, when local taxes are deductible on federal tax forms, the local "tax price" for all local services falls in the same way as the local price for specific programs falls under targeted matching grants. Although this does not allow the central government to

Table 3   Potential Efficiency-Enhancing Central Government
           Intervention under Federalism

Central Government Mandates	Regulation of permissible tax bases and rates	→ If properly constructed, may prevent the local tax externalities in table 2	State prohibitions against local income taxes
	Setting maximum and minimum levels of services	→ If properly set, may prevent the local spending externalities in table 1	TANF mandates that state governments must continue to maintain a fraction of pre-TANF welfare spending
Central Government Grants	Matching grants to lower tier	→ Can be constructed to internalize local externalities (tables 1 and 2) and to alleviate equity concerns	AFDC Matching formulas for local school financing (district power equalization)
	Deductibility of some local taxes	→ Can be used to encourage lower tiers to use certain tax bases, to internalize externalities, and to increase equity	U.S. deductibility of state income taxes and local property taxes
	Block grants	→ Large grants can centralize revenue collection while leaving spending decisions decentralized	TANF General revenue sharing

grants are often proposed on equity grounds when the equity standard is one of "equality of opportunity" rather than "equality of results."[19] Finally, although by themselves small block grants targeted at particular lower-tier activities are predicted to have little impact on the level of those activities (owing to the fungibility of such grants), large block grants are sometimes proposed when the central government seeks to take over the responsibility of financing the decentralized government activity while leaving specific spending decisions to state and local governments (Rivlin 1992). This last proposal is popular among many public finance economists because it allows the central government to ensure that spending levels are efficiently and equitably set, and lower-tier governments are given the flexibility to respond to local needs as well as to experiment with new policy ideas. All these policies, of course, are constrained by the extent to which the central government is able to collect sufficient information to determine which precise policies would lead to improvements in efficiency and equity.

We have now outlined the basic economic forces at work within a federal system under the simplifying assumption that all governments benevolently maximize public welfare within their jurisdictions. Under this assumption, a multitiered system of government has considerable advantages because different types of government services are best

---

change the relative local price *between different kinds of local government activities*, it does change the relative price *between local public spending and local private spending*. In the absence of statutory or constitutional tax base assignments, one potentially useful application of this might be to use *selective* tax deductibility of specific local taxes to encourage local governments to choose the "right" tax bases. See Nechyba (1996) for an illustration of the theoretical similarities between local tax deductibility and matching grants. (As discussed in the third section, however, political realities invalidate some of these theoretic similarities.)

19. In state education finance, for example, matching grants are one way to ensure that each school district, regardless of its property wealth, has the same opportunity to finance education (Feldstein 1975). One somewhat neglected constraint on the effectiveness of such grants arises if localities intentionally lower local tax bases via inefficient policies when local success implies a reduction in state or federal grants (see, for example, Hoxby [1997]).

provided by different levels of government. Because of the presence of externalities on both the expenditure and the tax sides and because of potential equity concerns over differential public service levels under decentralization, however, we suggested above that there is a potentially large role for central direction of local government activities within the federal system. In particular, we outlined how matching grants, large block grants, and central government mandates can serve to increase the efficiency of decentralized government behavior and to decrease equity problems that may arise with competing lower tiers. We now proceed to consider how these conclusions may change if we consider more-realistic assumptions regarding both central and local government behavior.

The Public Choice Literature on Federalism

Over the past few decades, economists have become increasingly cognizant of political science insights concerning government behavior. In particular, although economic models of governments as maximizers of public welfare provide important economic insights (such as those outlined earlier), real-world governments are subject to political pressures, interest group politics, election constraints, and bureaucratic incentives that may cause them to deviate substantially from the simple model we have employed thus far. Whereas the previous section investigated ways to alleviate "economic failures" when all governments act ideally, this section focuses on potential "political failures" when governments are modeled more realistically. Specifically, we ask two important questions: (1) what additional considerations regarding federalism enter under this new view of government behavior? and (2) how do our conclusions regarding optimal fiscal relations (grants and mandates) between central and lower-tier governments change in the face of nonoptimal government behavior?

SELF-INTERESTED GOVERNMENTS IN A FEDERAL SYSTEM

In the presence of political institutions that do not provide perfect incentives for politicians, governments invariably do not maximize consumer welfare.[20] Given the resulting government failures, we can therefore begin by asking whether federalism itself can improve political outcomes. There are at least two avenues by which this may occur: (1) just as monopoly rents disappear as an industry is subjected to competition, so political rents may decrease with increased lower-tier horizontal competition (Tiebout 1956) and (2) hierarchical competition as well as constitutional restraints on central governments may reduce inefficient government behavior and preserve markets that are fundamental to successful economic performance (Weingast 1993, 1995). The first of these provides a (political) argument for decentralization, and the second argues for strengthening restraints on central governments on the one hand and of competition throughout the federal system on the other. We briefly examine each of these in turn.

Earlier we introduced Tiebout's (1956) notion that a large number of competing communities may successfully introduce a market force into a system of governments by allowing individuals to "vote with their feet." In a system of lower-tier governments that maximizes public welfare within their jurisdictions, we demonstrated that this may make it considerably easier to satisfy diverse demands for public services as consumers self-segregate into communities on the basis of their tastes for public services. Now suppose that governments were the opposite of what we have assumed them to be thus far. In particular, suppose all governments were Leviathans (Brennan and Buchanan 1977)—revenue-maximizing or rent-seeking institutions—rather than benign maximizers of public welfare. It is then easy to see that the mobility of

---

20. See, among many others, Niskanen (1971), Brennan and Buchanan (1977), Weingast (1979), Shepsle (1979), and Baron and Ferejohn (1989) for examples of different approaches to modeling governments. Inman (1988a) provides an excellent overview of some of the most fundamental issues.

consumers adds an additional disciplining force on the lower-tier political process as residents simply abandon "bad" local governments that are not responsive to local needs and tastes.[21] In the absence of monetary considerations introduced in the next section, Tiebout competition therefore offers a way to lessen the ability of lower-tier governments to engage in rent seeking (and thus provides an additional decentralization force for table 1).

Riker (1964), however, warns that political forces at the center of the federal system may overawe lower-tier institutions as the center attempts to usurp local powers. This leads Weingast (1993) to conclude that federalism can maintain lower-tier political competition as well as credibly guarantee political and economic rights only so long as successful restraints on this centralizing tendency can be put into place. Appropriately designed federalism, known as *market-preserving federalism*, may then overcome what Weingast refers to as the "fundamental political dilemma of economic systems" that "a government strong enough to protect property rights is also strong enough to confiscate the wealth of its citizens." Formal as well as informal constraints on central government powers (hierarchical competition, constitutions as well as norms that support the rule of law) limit federal tendencies to seek political rents and to constrain political and economic rights, while Tiebout competition places similar limits on lower tiers. Weingast (1993, 1995) suggests that market-preserving federalism was a

---

21. Hoxby (1994) offers some interesting recent empirical evidence that competition among public school districts leads to increases in student achievement. The implicit conclusion one can draw from such a result is that increased competition leads to either a reduction in rent seeking or declines in bureaucratic inefficiencies of local school systems. A relatively large empirical literature testing the Leviathan assumption is still somewhat unsettled (see Eberts and Gronberg [1988], Marlow [1988], Zax [1989], Oates [1985, 1989], and references therein). Epple and Zelenitz (1981), however, demonstrate that the presence of fixed factors (like land) implies that rent seeking, if it exists, can never be completely eliminated through Tiebout competition and that politics within local governments introduces potential distortions even under perfect competition of lower-tier governments.

strong force in England (in the eighteenth century), the United States (in the nineteenth and twentieth centuries), and China over the past two decades.

IMPLICATIONS OF POLITICS FOR FISCAL FEDERALISM

Whereas the previous section argues that the introduction of politics generates additional arguments for the desirability of federalism as well as additional decentralizing forces that may cause us to assign more government activities to the lower tier, we now turn to the question of whether political realities could cause us to reevaluate the conclusions that emerge from the economics literature regarding the optimal fiscal relations between different tiers within a federalist system. In particular, recall that we concluded the second section by suggesting a number of tools (different kinds of mandates and grants) the central government could potentially use to increase the efficiency and equity properties of federal systems. We now suggest that, in the presence of more-realistic government institutions at the central and local levels, these tools are unlikely to be used in the efficiency and equity-enhancing ways suggested in table 3 because (1) the dominance of *distributive politics* in Congress and the likelihood of *unhealthy collusion* by lower tiers yield outcomes quite different from those suggested by public finance economists and (2) the informational constraints faced by voters cause federal interventions to result in a *loss of political accountability* of politicians to voters as well as an undesirable *loss of local autonomy*. All these forces lead to an unraveling of the very market-preserving features that we have argued are so attractive about federalism to begin with.

Local Government Collusion and Distributive Politics

First, note that the grants and mandates suggested in table 3 are intended to serve as a means for the *healthy* collusion of lower-tier governments in the face of lower-tier pressures that cause efficiency (or equity) problems. When lower-tier governments regulate ozone-depleting pollution, for example, we demonstrated that they will provide too little regulation and thus cause too much overall pollution. All jurisdictions therefore would be better off if they could collude and agree to take into consideration the benefit of their policies not only on their own citizens but also on the citizens elsewhere, but it is in each jurisdiction's interest to violate such an agreement unilaterally. Therefore, a central government can enforce such a healthy collusive agreement (either through mandate or grant incentives).

Once the central government is used as a means to achieve *healthy* collusion between lower-tier governments via annual legislation of grants and mandates, however, what will keep lower tiers from also using the center to collude in *unhealthy* ways? In particular, when nonbenign lower-tier governments find themselves under healthy competitive pressures (owing to the Tiebout forces described above), they can seek to reduce these pressures by agreeing to collude and having the central government act as an enforcer of their collusive agreements.[22] In the context of local government collusion, Nechyba (1997b), for example, suggests that *state* grants to school districts may have arisen as a way for local governments to use income taxes (rather than, or in addition to, property taxes) that competitive forces would have prevented in the absence of collusion. Such collusion, if achieved as a result of unhealthy local political pressures rather than healthy attempts to internalize externalities, undermines the desirable competitive pressures that local politicians would face in the absence of central government intervention.

---

22. The notion that governments can be used as enforcers of unhealthy collusive agreements is common to other areas in economics (see, for example, citations in Landsburg [1995] on regulations of private-sector industries). The need for collusion, as demonstrated in Nechyba (1997b), arises from the inherent "prisoner's dilemma" faced by lower-tier governments; while all prefer to collude to avoid competitive pressures, collusive agreements are not self-enforcing.

With respect to *federal* grant policies over the past thirty years, there is significant empirical evidence that collusive political behavior has caused these policies to deviate far from the ideals summarized in table 3.[23] Inman (1988b), for example, finds that federal grants to U.S. states cannot be explained on either equity or efficiency grounds but rather that they are the result of "distributive politics." Distributive politics essentially arises from a collusive political process in which lower-tier representatives behave in accordance with the old adage "you scratch my back, I'll scratch yours."[24] Political decisions in such an environment seek to concentrate benefits in specific geographic regions (electoral districts) while financing the cost of these benefits by spreading it over the general population. Thus, as argued in Inman and Rubinfeld (1996), distributive politics causes grant policies to be driven by *local* rather than national concerns and thus leads to substantial deviations from the national objectives suggested in table 3 and an overproduction of local (pork barrel) projects.[25]

---

23. Some notable exceptions exist, as, for example, Wildasin (1989) on deductibility of state capital taxes.

24. This notion is formally known as a "norm of deference" and explored in Weingast (1979) and Niou and Ordeshook (1985). Also, there is considerable empirical evidence suggesting that this characterizes congressional behavior on many issues, not just those dealing with national grants (see Weingast, Shepsle, and Johnson [1981] for references). For a lucid discussion of the history of U.S. legislative politics, see Shepsle and Weingast (1984).

25. The response of local governments to central government grants provides further evidence for this proposition. Although matching grants are effective in inducing local policy changes (as predicted by the theory), block grants prove more effective than expected in increasing local expenditures (Fischer 1996). This empirical phenomenon, known as the "flypaper effect," can be put more succinctly: when grants are given to lower-tier governments, local public expenditures rise much more than when the same amount of money is given to local voters in the form of tax cuts or deductions. Empirical estimates suggest that one dollar in a block grant results in an increase in lower-tier spending of between forty cents and one dollar, while a similar increase in income by local voters results in an increase of between five and ten cents (Hines and Thaler 1996). This is puzzling because the theory predicts that, whether grants are given directly to voters or indirectly to lower-tier governments, the outcome should be the similar if the local government acts in the interest of a representative (or median voter) resident.

Informational Constraints on the Part of Voters

Even in the absence of distributive politics and lower-tier political collusions, however, central government grant policies face serious real-world obstacles arising from information barriers faced by voters. It is a well-known proposition among policy analysts, for example, that the efficiency of a system that relies on voters to keep politicians accountable is directly related to the simplicity of that system (see, for example, discussions on tax reform in Boskin [1996] and Aaron and Gale [1996]). For our purposes, voters at each level of government within a federal system must know both how much in tax revenues a particular level collected and what services that level provided in order to judge whether the tax money was used parsimoniously. A complicated system of grants and mandates, however, obscures the taxpayer's perception of how much is being done at each level of government with what resources. The sharing of government responsibilities as well as joint financing of those activities therefore enables politicians at different levels of government to "pass the buck" and makes it difficult for voters to know which politicians to hold accountable.[26]

Similarly, with less than perfect information on the part of voters, the general argument (contained in various elements of table 3) that central financing of lower-tier activities may be efficiency enhancing presumes a great deal of restraint on the part of central government politicians. In particular, if voters are unable to follow the "money trail" in the federal grant system, the argument assumes that central govern-

---

Although economists have posited numerous possible economic explanations for this phenomenon, none of them has proven to be particularly empirically relevant (Wyckoff 1991). Ultimately, the answer to this puzzle is also likely to point in the direction of inefficient distributive politics or behavioral explanations that point to equally inefficient political outcomes (Hines and Thaler 1996).

26. A good illustration of this was provided in the 1988 campaign in which George Bush ran advertisements attacking the governor of Massachusetts for the pollution in Boston Harbor, while the same governor used the same issue to suggest that the Reagan/Bush administration had been negligent in its federal environmental policy.

ment politicians will accept the political pain of raising taxes without receiving the political payoff of determining how the resulting revenues are to be spent. Historically, this has simply not been the case. Most often, central government politicians will use the financial leverage they have under a grant system to mandate various policies that lower tiers themselves would not have chosen. The Reagan administration, for example, used federal highway funding for states as a means to coerce states to raise the drinking age from eighteen to twenty-one. Similarly, programs like AFDC and Medicaid (which were technically administered by state governments and funded, at least in part, by the central government) have experienced a declining level of state participation as federal mandates increased. Given that such mandates allow federal politicians to be be seen as doing something about various policy problems without having to undertake any additional taxation, it is not surprising that federal *funding* inevitably leads to federal *control*. Similarly, in the financing of public education, a move toward central funding at the state level has generally also entailed a decline in local control over school policies (see, for example, the California experience). Thus, although shared financing of lower-tier responsibilities may in principle be efficiency enhancing by allowing both the benefits of decentralization and local autonomy (local information) and the benefits of centralization (externality and equity concerns) to coexist, the *central control that typically comes with central government involvement* makes this impractical in many applications.

In light of these political distortions (summarized in table 4), there is thus considerable doubt whether a central government can be relied on to pursue efficiency-enhancing grants and mandates consistently and whether lower-tier governments will respond to these incentives as expected. The *pervasiveness of distributive politics* at the legislative level and the potential for *unhealthy collusion* through central government direction combined with the *loss of political accountability and local autonomy* that comes with increased intergovernmental fiscal

Table 4   Potential Political Distortions under Federalism

Distortions Arising from Nonbenign Local Politics	Local desire to curtail (healthy) competition	→ Central government mandates and grants can be used as enforcement mechanisms for collusive agreements	Income tax–funded state grants to lower tiers that cannot use such taxes owing to competitive pressures
	Distributive politics ("you scratch my back, I'll scratch yours")	→ Central government direction is motivated by local, not national, concerns	Federal grants for concentrated local benefits (pork barrel projects)
Further Distortions Owing to Imperfect Information by Voters	Complexity of federal interventions	→ Uncertainty over who is in charge causes political shirking and lack of accountability	Environmental policy (Boston Harbor) State school finance
	Lack of central government restraint	→ Inability by center to raise taxes for local spending without attaching strings causes loss of local autonomy under grants	Centralization of public school financing typically results in centralization of public school policy

interactions suggests to us that those recommendations in table 3 that rely on annual legislative action are not politically feasible despite their economic potential under benevolent government behavior. We therefore conclude that a healthy federal system (in the absence of problems due to monetary constraints raised in the next section) ought to constitutionally assign government services and tax bases to different levels and then to allow each level to operate with relatively little additional central direction. Although this limits the role of the central government in terms of annual tinkering with the system, it places a large emphasis on constitutional design.[27] We turn to more specifics in the final section after considering the complications introduced by the presence of monetary institutions and constraints.

The Monetary System, Borrowing Constraints, and Intergenerational Equity

Surprisingly, both the traditional theory of federalism, with benevolent governments striving to maximize the welfare of their residents, and the public choice literature extolling interjurisdictional competition to restrain rent-seeking behavior by imperfect governments generally fail to analyze borrowing constraints on governments themselves. Both approaches presume that any government's spending is limited by its tax revenues (possibly supplemented by grants-in-aid). But, as we shall show in this section, this presumption of a *hard restraint on borrowing* is only valid if that government is suitably separated from the monetary mechanism.

From this capital-market perspective, a *potential* major advantage of a federal system is that many—if not most—public goods and services can be provided by middle- and lower-level governments that have hard borrowing constraints because they are separated from the monetary system. For example, U.S. states (and municipalities) cannot issue much general-purpose debt for covering current consumption without being downgraded in the credit markets. The credit market protects the future generation from encroachment by limiting government borrowing to capital improvements. Similarly, we shall also show that the efficiency of horizontal Tiebout competition is enhanced

---

27. Inman (1988b) shows that strong political parties may also be able to reduce inefficient grant spending, and he suggests that executive veto threats have been used effectively in the past (under the Reagan administration). For a law and economics perspective on tax base assignments, see Shaviro (1992).

when middle-level governments have hard borrowing constraints and may be counterproductive when these budget constraints are soft.

SOURCES OF GOVERNMENT DEBT AND
INTERGENERATIONAL TRANSFERS

The borrowing proclivities of governments, in or out of federal systems, vary enormously. In the industrial countries today, the big issue in public finance is the question of intergenerational equity: the buildup of claims on future generations who are not represented in today's electoral processes. Since the late 1970s, the buildup of general-purpose public debt, largely used to finance current consumption, has been one way of shifting costs to future generation(s). Table 5 shows debt accumulation by nineteen national governments in Western Europe, North America, and Japan. On average, gross debt rose from 40.4 percent of gross domestic product (GDP) in 1978 to 72.4 percent in 1995.[28]

This problem of imperfect governance (i.e., the failure to protect the future) would seem to be a natural topic for analysis by the public choice literature. After all, writers in this vein worry about political accountability and the ambit of government. Rather than borrowing per se, however, the public choice literature has focused on restraints—constitutional or through intergovernmental competition—on taxation (Brennan and Buchanan 1977; Weingast 1993). This theme was picked up by President Reagan's supply-siders in the 1980s, who wanted to limit government simply by cutting taxes.

However, political restraints on taxation need not restrict, and may even encourage, government borrowing, as was the case with the explosion in U.S. federal debt in the 1980s. But at the level of U.S. states

---

28. More difficult to calculate is the buildup of unfunded Social Security liabilities. The International Monetary Fund estimates (May 1996) that these net Social Security liabilities are of the same order of magnitude as the debt overhangs shown in table 5.

Table 5   Gross Public Debt (as a percentage of nominal GDP) [a]

	1978	1988	1993	1995
United States	39.2%	52.7%	63.9%	64.3%
Japan	41.9	70.6	74.7 [b]	81.3
Germany	30.1	44.4	48.5	61.6
France	31.0	40.6	52.5	57.9
Italy	62.4	94.8	118.4	123.0
United Kingdom	58.6	42.2	56.9	57.6
Canada	46.6	69.2	92.3	99.1
Total of above countries	*41.6*	*57.8*	*67.1*	*71.9*
Australia [c]	—	27.3	33.9	43.8
Austria [d]	33.9	57.6	57.0	73.9
Belgium	70.4	132.1	137.9	133.5
Denmark [d]	21.9	68.2	86.0	80.1
Finland [d]	13.5	19.6	59.5	63.0
Greece [d]	29.4	71.1	111.7	111.5
Ireland	65.7	113.0	97.3	85.8
Netherlands	40.2	76.2	81.0	79.1
Norway [d]	60.0	35.1	43.3	39.7
Portugal	37.6	65.0	67.5 [b]	70.7
Spain [d]	14.4	46.9	65.8	71.1
Sweden	34.5	53.5	76.3	81.8
Total of above European countries	*41.0*	*57.9*	*67.4*	*76.3*
Total for all countries	*40.4*	*58.1*	*67.4*	*72.4*

[a] Refers to general government debt. Note that the definition of debt applied under the Maastricht Treaty differs from the national accounts definitions used by the Organization for Economic Cooperation and Development (OECD).

[b] OECD Secretariat estimates starting from 1993.

[c] Debt data refer to fiscal years ending June 30 and include indebtedness of local government toward other levels of general government.

[d] Does not exclude public-sector mutual indebtedness.

and municipalities, no such explosion occurred even though they too were often subject to the influence of the supply-siders. Despite the huge ebb and flow of the debt/gross national product (GNP) ratio of the U.S. federal government for the last several decades, the outstanding debt positions of the states and municipalities have remained remarkably constant (see table 6).[29] In contrast, the current political push

29. Table 6 shows state plus local debt as a share of GNP that has remained stable

Table 6   U.S. Government Gross Debt: Federal, State, and Local
           (as a percentage of GNP)

Year	Total	Federal	State+Local	State	Local
1929	32.1%	16.3%	15.9%	2.2%	13.7%
1939	66.3	44.2	2.2	3.8	18.2
1949	105.1	97.7	8	1.5	6.5
1954	83.1	72.7	10.5	2.6	7.9
1959	70.4	57.4	12.9	3.4	9.5
1964	62.9	48.8	14.1	3.8	10.3
1965	59.3	45.2	14.1	3.8	10.3
1970	50.9	36.7	14.3	4.2	10.1
1975	48.3	34.3	13.9	4.5	9.4
1980	46.2	33.8	12.4	4.5	7.9
1985	59.4	45.2	14.1	5.2	8.9
1986	65.3	49.9	15.4	5.8	9.6
1987	67.7	51.9	15.9	5.9	10
1988	68.8	53.4	15.4	5.6	9.8
1989	70.1	54.9	15.2	5.6	9.6
1990	74.7	59.1	15.6	5.8	9.8
1991	81.1	65.0	16.2	6.1	10.1
1992	83.7	67.6	16.1	6.2	9.9

SOURCE: Advisory Commission on Intergovernmental Relations (ACIR), *Significant Features of Fiscal Federalism* (Washington, D.C.: U.S. Government Printing Office, 1994).

NOTE: Gross debt used by the ACIR differs somewhat from the OECD and Maastricht definitions.

in Congress for a balanced-budget amendment reflects the perception that market-imposed restraints on the U.S. federal government's ability to issue debt are weak indeed. In fact, U.S. general government debt rose from 39.2 percent of GNP in 1978 to 64.3 percent in 1995, a rate of increase similar to most other national governments in the OECD (see table 5). Why the capital markets prevent *some* governments from borrowing against the future (e.g., U.S. state-level governments), while

---

at about 16 percent of GNP between 1929 and the early 1990s. General-purpose state debt, which is not clearly associated with capital improvements, remains about 6 percent of GNP. Local bond issues, which are associated with capital improvements, remain about 10 percent of GNP.

others were hardly disciplined at all (e.g., national governments every-where in the industrial world since the early 1970s), has been ad-dressed neither by the public choice literature nor by the traditional benevolent-government theory of public finance. The precise mone-tary and fiscal conditions for sustaining hard borrowing constraints that enable capital markets to effectively discipline governments therefore remain to be spelled out.

A MONETARY THEORY OF GOVERNMENT BORROWING CONSTRAINTS

Although there is a vast literature on how fiscal policy may ulti-mately determine the money supply and rate of inflation (Sargent and Wallace 1981), little has been written on how monetary institutions themselves may constrain governments from issuing nonmonetary debt. The theory presented here was developed by McKinnon (1994, 1995, 1996a, 1996b, and 1997), with interesting applications to China by Montinola, Qian, and Weingast (1994).[30] The basic idea behind this theory is that any government (federal, state/provincial, or local) faces a hard borrowing constraint if each of the following conditions is satisfied: (1) monetary separation, (2) fiscal separation, and (3) freedom of interstate commerce (mobility). These conditions are necessary for unrestricted local public choice (within the framework of a proper assignment of tax and spending authorities) to operate effectively, and this unrestricted public choice further reinforces the hardness of bud-get constraints.

Monetary Separation

Monetary separation means that, in a fiat money system, the gov-ernment in question does not have access to the central bank, nor does

---

30. Ragan (in McKinnon [1996b]) greatly helped simplify the theory presented below.

it own or strongly influence commercial banks that could borrow (receive discount loans) from the central bank. When the national government owns its own central bank, everyone in the economy realizes that, in a crisis, the government can always "print money" (i.e., use the inflation tax) to pay interest and principal and thus avoid outright default on the face value of its obligations. Because easy (potential) access to monetary seigniorage greatly reduces any risk of outright default, the government that owns the central bank can preempt the national capital market to issue treasury securities at lower interest rates than can high-quality private borrowers whose debt is also denominated in the national currency. Unlike the national government, private companies are subject to commercial risk (i.e., the threat of bankruptcy). And holders of private securities face the same inflation risk as do holders of claims on the national government.

Consequently, in any country with an independent fiat money system,[31] central government bonds are considered to be the safest financial instruments denominated in the national currency.[32] Because the U.S. federal government thus has a "soft" budget constraint on issuing debt ex ante, it also has very high debt outstanding ex post—just as do other national governments that also have the highest credit rating in their own respective national capital markets. In contrast, U.S. state governments neither own nor influence the Federal Reserve Bank and have long since lost the power to charter note-issuing commercial

---

31. The situation could be quite different if there were an external convertibility constraint on domestic money issue, as under a full-fledged gold standard like that prevailing before 1914. Then national governments, even if they owned their own central banks, were highly constrained in their ability to issue debt to cover current consumption (i.e., they were effectively disciplined by the capital markets).

32. In the United States, the highest-grade Aaa corporate bonds usually pay an interest rate a percentage point or so higher than on long-term U.S. Treasury bonds; B-grade corporate bonds pay about 2 percentage points higher; and unrated "junk" bonds may pay 3 to 4 percentage points or more. After allowing for tax differences, interest on the debt of U.S. state and local governments is also substantially higher than that on federal debt.

banks or to force commercial banks to lend to them.[33] Thus, as long as they remain fiscally independent (to be described below), lower-tier budgets in the United States are significantly "harder," and state and municipal bonds carry significant default risk on interest and principal. When issued in domestic U.S. capital markets, state bonds are then subject to the same strict credit ratings as private bond issues.[34]

Fiscal Separation

When the government in question does not receive residual finance from other governments, especially higher-level ones with central banks, through redistributive revenue sharing or equalization grants, there is *fiscal separation*, without which the soft borrowing constraints of the national governments would be transmitted downward to middle and local governments. If the capital markets knew that the national government would rescue any local government in distress, even if only in the ex ante sense of coming up with a more generous revenue-sharing plan or an equalization grant to head off a crisis, they would lend more to that government before its credit rating fell ex post.

In Canada, for example, the federal government's finances are much more entangled with those of the provinces than in the United States (Courchene 1994). Poorer provinces like Newfoundland and Nova Scotia receive large, ongoing direct equalization grants as well as more than their pro rata share from income and sales taxes collected for them by the federal government. Consequently, the financial markets have been less worried about borrowing by Canadian provinces because provincial governments appear to be a financial extension of

---

33. This is in contrast to Brazilian state governments, which own large commercial banks that have generous discount privileges with the Brazilian central bank. Argentinean state governments have traditionally leaned heavily on banks they own or influence to borrow excessively.

34. In 1994, eight states were rated Aaa, but others ranged from A (New York) down to Baa1 (Louisiana).

the federal government. Although the range of Moody's bond ratings for Canadian provinces is similar to that for U.S. states, in recent years the provinces have built up debts about twice as high as U.S. state and municipal debts combined.

What key features of the U.S. federal system preserve effective fiscal separation in the eyes of the financial markets? Joint state-federal programs in the areas of medical assistance to the poor (Medicaid), managing unemployment benefits, welfare as with ADFC and TANF discussed above, along with matching grants for local school financing and unfunded mandates that the federal government may impose on schools and localities, have been around for many years. Because of numerous state-federal programs, some of which are summarized in table 3, at first glance fiscal separation in the United States hardly seems robust.

Nevertheless, these entitlement programs are all fairly tightly specified in terms of eligibility of the beneficiaries. Until the 1996 switch from AFDC to TANF, the state governments had little discretion in administering these programs and federal monies did not flow to each state as such. Rather, federal matching grants could only be collected as beneficiaries showed up to claim benefits. So, unlike Canadian equalization grants to the provinces, the U.S. federal government did not give general grants to, say, the state of Mississippi just because it was poor. (Nevertheless, an inappropriate expansion of a new system of block grants from the federal government to the states could undermine this fiscal separation and inadvertently soften state borrowing constraints in the future, as we analyze in the final section below.)

On the tax side, the U.S. Constitution gives the states sovereign authority to raise revenues as they see fit as long as they do not tax foreign trade or interstate commerce per se. Each state has developed its own administration for collecting income, sales, or even property taxes, which are all specified independently of federal tax liabilities. Thus, there is little pooling of revenues between the state and federal governments and no transfers to the states (or from one state to another) in large measure because each state government collects its own taxes and remains fiscally independent. Effective fiscal separation therefore exists in the sense that the capital markets do not view the U.S. federal government as a source of residual finance to, or the ultimate guarantor of, the state governments, and any state or locality could go bankrupt without causing the center to intervene.[35]

Freedom of Interstate Commerce (Mobility)

Together, our first two conditions—direct monetary separation and fiscal separation that prevents middle-level governments from having indirect access to the central bank—imply that borrowing constraints on states and localities will be "virtually" hard. That is, the financial markets will be reluctant to finance current deficits, although they will still finance self-liquidating capital-account expenditures. If the government has an unchallenged tax monopoly in a jurisdiction of immobile taxpayers, however, its borrowing constraints may not be completely hard in that there remains a possibility of shifting debt to future generations. To limit this possibility and to enhance the efficiency of

---

35. Bayoumi and Eichengreen (1994) estimate that a state with a current fiscal deficit will be downgraded in the credit markets and that, if nothing is done to staunch the fiscal hemorrhage, the errant state would be rationed out of the capital markets altogether when general-purpose debt reaches a fairly modest 10 percent or so of state gross product. Furthermore, the rather narrow and specialized nature of the market for U.S. state and local bonds seems to contribute to this very hard borrowing constraint. Because interest paid on state and local bonds is exempt from U.S. federal income taxation, wealthy individuals resident in the United States become the principal buyers and the equilibrium nominal interest rates are significantly less—about 2 percentage points—than on U.S. Treasury or high-grade corporate bonds. Thus foreigners, who would not receive the tax advantage, do not buy them, and the market becomes narrowly "onshore" in U.S. dollars. This makes it easier for the U.S. federal government to ignore bankruptcies in any one state or locality (i.e., no bailout) because any such bankruptcy does not impair the country's international credit rating or the credit standing of the other states. In contrast, bonds of the Canadian provinces are marketed in a variety of other countries and currencies at current interest rates. Thus, should any one province default, the Canadian federal government may well worry more about the contagion effects on the credit ratings of the others.

intergovernmental tax competition, we add the condition *freedom of interstate commerce* (i.e., no restraints on the movement of goods, business firms, people, or capital across jurisdictions).[36]

HARD BUDGET CONSTRAINTS AND THE COMMITMENT
TO MARKET-PRESERVING PUBLIC CHOICE

Under what conditions, then, is *unrestricted public choice* (i.e., no restrictions on domestic taxation for financing local public goods and for competing with other jurisdictions to attract industry, labor, or capital) both feasible and desirable? More specifically, in a federal system, under what conditions can the central government commit itself to a hands-off policy as middle-level governments compete vigorously through tax and expenditure policy for resources? We shall argue that the conditions of monetary separation, fiscal separation, and free trade (see table 7) are necessary constraints for general competition among middle-level governments to be market preserving while preventing undue shifting of debt burdens to the future. When they are satisfied that borrowing constraints are hard, and when government activities and tax bases have been assigned appropriately (according to the criteria laid out in tables 1 and 2), competition among governments takes on the healthy characteristics of competitive markets in general. Thus, the three conditions in table 7 may also be sufficient for the central government to commit itself to respecting the sovereignty of middle governments making their own tax and expenditure decisions. If they can compete with one another without regulatory interference from the center, unrestricted public choice is sustainable. Conversely, if the borrowing constraints on the middle- and lower-level governments are

---

36. A potential major advantage of a federal system is that the central government is well placed to enforce complete freedom of interstate commerce within the country—as provided for in the U.S. Constitution. In contrast, independent nation-states must negotiate complex international trade agreements that usually fall short of this ideal.

Table 7   Conditions for Intergenerationally Efficient Competition
               among State Governments

Monetary Separation	No access to central bank and no ownership or strong influence of commercial banks	→ Lack of an ability to "print money" removes *direct* distortionary advantage in capital markets	U.S. state governments have no monetary authority (as opposed to nation-states in the European Union [EU])
Fiscal Separation	No grant revenues from higher-tier governments (who have access to central banks)	→ fiscal disconnection from the higher tier that has the ability to "print money" removes *indirect* distortionary advantage	U.S. federal grants have historically been much more limited in scope than, for example, Canadian federal grants
Freedom of Commerce under appropriate assignment of government activities	No government barriers to interjurisdictional mobility of goods, factors, and residents	→ Removes final distortion in credit markets by removing the guarantee of future tax revenues from "captive" populations	Freedom of interstate commerce is guaranteed by the U.S. Constitution, and cultural barriers are lower than in the EU

soft, horizontal tax and expenditure competition among them may be sufficiently destructive that the center may feel compelled to intervene continually *even if all assignments of government activities and tax bases have been made appropriately.*[37]

To illustrate this point, consider the consequences of mercantile competition among European nation-states, which have historically had (at least before European monetary unification [EMU]) soft borrowing constraints, thus violating our monetary separation condition.

---

37. To what extent central governments can successfully accomplish this, given the political constraints raised earlier, however, is not clear.

Because each national government owns the central bank, each government cannot be sufficiently constrained from borrowing to finance current consumption—including bailing out loss-making state-owned enterprises. Consequently, free horizontal tax and expenditure competition among European governments is problematic (McKinnon 1995) just as unrestricted public choice was problematic, as discussed earlier, when government responsibilities and tax bases have not been assigned so as to internalize externalities.[38] Similarly, if future benefits are not properly weighed under soft borrowing constraints, national governments may engage in the same type of "beggar-thy-neighbor" policies that arise in table 2 under unhealthy tax competition when tax bases are not properly assigned.[39]

In striking contrast to Europe, the U.S. federal government generally ignores the ebb and flow of equally vigorous mercantile competition among the states. Despite sporadic attempts by states to engage in unhealthy competition of the type seen in Europe, their hard borrowing constraints prevent them from systematically subsidizing uneconomic activities or shifting debt burdens to the future, and the freedom-of-interstate-commerce clause in the Constitution prevents the states from trying to keep out one another's goods or restrict factor movements.[40]

---

38. Thus, the EU commission has always been in the uncomfortable position of having to promulgate rules to preserve markets because national governments will inefficiently subsidize national industrial champions.

39. The resulting debt burdens from such policies are shifted to future generations who are not participating in today's political process. This is most easily seen when loss-making enterprises are simply recapitalized; the national government assumes responsibility for the bonds of the failing company in return for equity of dubious quality. European airlines, such as Air France and Iberia, have gone through several such recapitalizations. Although the EU commission does its best to curb this politically poisonous type of intergovernmental competition, it is an uphill struggle.

40. These two conditions reinforce each other. State governments, whose ability to tax now or in the future is limited by the threat of competition from other states, find it more difficult to borrow to finance current (but not capital) expenditures. The credit markets will be skeptical about the repayment capabilities of any state government that

BACKWARD AREAS

One concern regarding fiscal separation is that it may limit the national government from aiding economically distressed regions within the country. A hallmark of European and Canadian fiscal policies, therefore, is the idea that intergovernmental equalization grants or tax breaks for poor areas are essential national policy instruments. It is appropriate, then, to ask whether unrestricted horizontal competition among the hard-budget American state governments would not simply lead to the rich getting richer and the poor getting poorer?

Experience seems to suggest otherwise. As late as 1950, the relative poverty of the southern American states was thought to be endemic. But by making their labor markets more flexible and by setting less generous welfare provisions, resulting in lower payroll taxes than in the northern states, southern states began to attract private corporate investment on a vast scale, and by the 1970s, much of the formerly backward region had become the prosperous Sunbelt. In striking contrast, regional equalization grants in Europe and Canada seem to have impeded this natural process of "equalization through competition" (McKinnon 1997). Within Italy, for example, huge transfer payments from the rich North to the poor South—the Mezzogiorno—have amounted to about 10 percent of Italian GNP for several decades. But the Mezzogiorno remains depressed and evermore welfare dependent. Similarly, for several decades, the poor Maritime provinces of Canada have received huge transfers from the central government without narrowing the income gap with the rest of Canada (Courchene 1994). In both these cases, it appears that the large intergovernmental transfer payments financed generous unemployment and other social benefits

---

tries to finance its current spending by borrowing—particularly if that errant government must compete in issuing debt with similar governments whose budgets are in better shape.

in the poorer areas that inhibited their labor markets from adjusting in the Amerian mode.

Policy Implications and Conclusions

Both the public finance and the public choice perspectives discussed earlier find persuasive arguments suggesting that federalism, *if properly designed*, offers substantial advantages over unitary governments, but the two perspectives differ on their recommendations as to what a proper design entails. Although it is difficult to disagree with the general public finance assertion that externalities (tax and spending) as well as potential inequities will arise in any federal system regardless of how carefully it is designed, it is not immediately clear to what extent the standard public finance recommendation of central grants and mandates can alleviate these problems. In particular, public choice theory warns of undesirable and unintended consequences, given that such central government policies are generated through a set of imperfect political institutions. Monetary theory suggests that large fiscal interactions between a central government (in charge of monetary policy) and lower tiers may have adverse impacts on intergenerational efficiency (and equity), as well as introduce nonbenign forces into otherwise healthy horizontal competition between lower-tier governments. We now proceed to use these insights to discuss current policies as well as the broader issues surrounding the optimal design of federal institutions.

ASSIGNMENT OF ACTIVITIES AND TAX BASES

We begin with the problem of using the principles laid out in table 1 to assign responsibilities and tax bases to three stylized tiers of government: local, state, and central. In the absence of equity concerns, government services that have few geographic spillovers and those that rely heavily on local tastes and information ought to be provided by local governments. Clear examples of such services (outlined in table 8) include *intra*community transportation and infrastructure, municipal police (for crimes with no spatial spillovers) and fire services, neighborhood parks and recreational activities (such as fireworks), local trash collection, and, in the United States, public education.[41] Equity concerns, however, are present for some of these services, in particular public schooling. These concerns have caused some analysts (as well as many state courts) to argue that services such as public education ought to be more centralized, but we remain persuaded at this point that local parental input in education is of such paramount importance that, with some state financial assistance, which we discuss below, education ought to remain a locally provided public service. Government activities that involve larger geographic spillovers but do not yet give rise to nationally felt externalities, in contrast, ought to be provided by a middle tier we call *states*. (Table 8 lists some examples of such services.) Furthermore, to the extent that public demand for redistributive policies differs widely between states, state governments may play a potentially large role in supplementing federal redistributive efforts. Northeastern states like Massachusetts, for example, have a demonstrably larger propensity to redistribute than many southern states like Louisiana. Given that greater income equality and lower poverty have primarily local effects, it is plausible for different states to have quite different redistributive policies. Finally, activities with nationally felt externalities, such as those outlined in table 8, are best handled by the central government.[42] Similarly, to the extent to which there exists national consensus on a minimum federal "safety net," federal

---

41. As suggested earlier, Wyckoff (1996) provides evidence that spillovers in public education are minor.

42. In a chapter in this volume, Richard Revesz, however, demonstrates that we may sometimes overestimate the extent to which the federal political process can effectively deal even with these types of government activities.

Table 8   Assignments of Specific Responsibilities

	Government Activities	Tax Bases
Central Tier	On efficiency grounds Macroeconomic policy National defense and international affairs Federal crime policy (for crimes with large interstate spillovers) Some types of environmental regulation, antitrust regulation, and consumer protection On equity grounds Interpersonal redistribution	On efficiency grounds Personal income [a] Corporate income (if taxed separately) Tariffs On equity grounds Progressive income tax rates
Middle Tier	On efficiency grounds Intrastate/intercommunity transportation and other state infrastructure State crime and corrections policy Judicial protection of property rights Public pensions State parks and recreation State universities Some types of environmental regulation and consumer/worker protection On equity grounds Interpersonal redistribution to supplement central government safety net Foundation aid for local education	On efficiency grounds Sales taxes [b] Nonresidential property tax [c] User fees (when possible)
Lower Tier	On efficiency grounds Primary and secondary education Intracommunity transportation and other infrastructure Municipal police and fire services Neighborhood parks/recreation/libraries	On efficiency grounds Residential land and property taxes User fees

[a] Owing to space considerations, we do not take a position here as to the precise definition of income to be used.

[b] We favor explicit sales taxes over value-added taxes (VATs) because of the hidden nature of the VAT (political accountability) and the burdensome requirement of border stations for tax collection.

[c] Apportionment of this tax may be necessary in some instances to overcome the not-in-my-backyard phenomenon.

interpersonal redistribution through both tax and spending policies is appropriate (to be supplemented by state redistributive programs that reflect differential tastes for local redistribution).

On the tax side, the principles summarized in table 2 determine the optimal assignment of tax bases to different tiers. At the local level, the various potential tax externalities are strongest because of the mobility of residents and factors among jurisdictions. Thus, it is important to find bases that are relatively immobile (to prevent unhealthy tax competition)[43] and that ensure that taxation is *resident* (not source) based (to prevent tax exporting). Out of the three broad tax systems we can choose from (property, sales, and income taxation), the one that best satisfies these requirements is the *residential* property tax.[44] Nonresidential property taxes, however, are more easily exported because land (and certain improvements on land) represents a fixed factor in the production of export goods.[45] Furthermore, local taxation of com-

---

43. To the extent that relatively immobile bases are taxed at the local level, this does permit rent seeking by local governments (Epple and Zelenitz 1981) and allows some softening of local budgets. With sufficient mobility of residents and other factors, however, these effects are still quite limited.

44. In fact, if residents are mobile and local governments use residential zoning effectively, residential property taxation becomes the only real-world tax that is fully efficient (Hamilton 1975, 1976). There is, however, large disagreement over the extent to which these conditions are satisfied (see Mieszkowski and Zodrow [1989] and Fischel [1992] for a recent version of this debate). In particular, if housing capital is highly mobile, the property tax becomes a mix of an inefficient excise and profits (capital) tax (Mieszkowski 1972). Thus, the efficiency argument for property taxation as well as the extent to which tax competition at the local level (under property taxes) is efficiency enhancing rests on the prevalence of zoning, the mobility of residents, and the relative immobility of housing capital. McLure(1986) argues persuasively, however, that perhaps the precise effects of the property tax are not as important as the decline in rent seeking that likely results from competition under either view. Furthermore, there is greater agreement on the efficiency of taxes on unimproved land, but it is often difficult to distinguish between the part of "property value" that is due to such land and the part that is due to improvements on land (housing). Finally, Nechyba (1997b) demonstrates that property taxation may in fact be the only potential local tax system that is politically and economically stable.

45. Of course, the final row of table 2 should be kept in mind as well.

mercial/industrial property would lead to the "beggar-thy-neighbor" policies discussed earlier. Thus, such taxation is usually best undertaken at the state level, but at least some of the revenues thus collected may have to be returned to local governments as compensation (to prevent the NIMBY phenomenon from table 2) if certain industries have particularly harmful local effects (landfills).

Similarly, sales taxes are problematic at the local level because "cross-border shopping" (which results in unhealthy tax competition) is relatively costless when jurisdictions are geographically small. Although such cross-border shopping is still possible at the state level, it is more difficult for consumers and thus less of a problem. Furthermore, cross-border shopping gives rise to the generally healthy consequence that states are constrained to keep sales taxes relatively uniform on all goods because excessive taxation of any one good beyond a certain level would result in loss of tax revenues. Since broad tax bases and low marginal tax rates are typically more efficient than narrow bases and high rates, as long as cross-border shopping does not give rise to excessive, unhealthy tax competition (as it would if sales taxes were administered by geographically small districts), the "tax base broadening" effect of competition at the state level may outweigh the remaining negative impact of unhealthy tax competition. For this reason, we assign sales taxes[46] to middle-tier governments in table 8.[47]

Finally, we assign the income tax to the central government for

---

46. We also prefer explicit sales taxation to value-added taxation (VAT) because sales taxation is not "hidden" to voters and because of subtle yet burdensome problems that arise owing to a lack of border stations for tax collections.

47. Inman and Rubinfeld (1996) argue that resident-based income taxation that is "piggybacked" on the federal income tax also represents an attractive state tax base assignment. States have, in fact, had the option to piggyback on the federal income tax system (i.e., have the federal government collect state taxes using the same definitions of taxable income), but no state has exercised this option (Strauss 1990). We think this may in part be due to the inherent suspicion on the part of states that intermingling their finances with the federal tax forms may lead to additional federal constraints later on. For this reason, we, too, are skeptical in regard to the piggyback definition of state tax bases.

two reasons: (1) mobility of labor and capital gives rise to unhealthy tax competition at the lower tiers, and (2) the income tax is particularly amenable to the central government concern over interpersonal equity in that it can easily be structured into a national safety net. Neither sales nor property taxes are easily turned into such an instrument.[48]

INTERGOVERNMENTAL GRANTS AND MANDATES

Although we agree with the public finance assertion that any federal system will be subject to equity and efficiency problems, we also conclude that the historical evidence supports the public choice view that central government policies that rely on legislative actions have generally not corrected for these problems and are unlikely to do so in the future. Furthermore, since the central government (at least in the United States) has control over monetary institutions and thus makes policy subject to a soft budget constraint, the standard tool of intergovernmental grants may be particularly dangerous and give rise to new intergenerational inefficiencies and inequities. This is why we think the proper assignment of tax bases and responsibilities is so crucial; once these assignments have been made, central government political institutions seem ill equipped to improve on them, especially in light of soft central budget constraints. Thus central direction of federal systems is most likely to lead to public finance objectives if institutionalized via a constitutional division of powers that internalizes externalities in the ways suggested in the previous section.

Whereas we are thus generally skeptical of the use of intergovernmental grants and mandates (beyond constitutional assignments), there may be circumstances under which such grants, on a limited

---

48. Although we favor incorporating the corporate income tax into the personal income tax (McLure 1975; Hall and Rabushka 1995), if there is to be a separate corporate income tax, we suggest that it be handled at the national, not the state, level for reasons outlined in McLure (1980).

basis, are appropriate. Under the current welfare reform, for example, federal welfare responsibilities for specific programs are being passed to state governments but are subsidized through large block grants. The passing of such responsibilities to states seems healthy in that a "race to the bottom" is unlikely (see the chapter by Volden in this volume) and in that there is potential for innovation at the state level. Furthermore, the use of block grants may well represent a onetime "payoff" by the central government to states to compensate them for their additional responsibilities. If, however, the system of block grants becomes a permanent link between federal and state entities, several potential dangers emerge: (1) the benefits from state responsiveness to local needs and from state innovation may be eroded by the tendency of the center in each fiscal year to attach further "strings" to the grants; (2) voters may have difficulty holding politicians accountable, as it is unclear who is in charge of welfare (or other block-granted) policies; and (3) state government budgets may soften to the point where serious indebtedness at the state level could result in substantial intergenerational equity problems. For these reasons, we suggest that federal block grants be used as transitional tools, *not as permanent institutions to govern lower-tier behavior*. Similar arguments apply to matching grants unless they are specifically targeted to well-identified and measurable state externalities.[49]

As long as state budgets are kept "hard" under relative fiscal separation from the center, however, the fear of lower-tier budgets softening as a result of intergovernmental grants disappears when we consider state (rather than federal) grants to local governments. To what extent, then, do we see a role for grants from state to local governments? Although we continue to view the evidence as suggesting that public choice barriers make annual efficiency-enhancing interventions by states generally not feasible, we do think there exist situations under

49. For alternative views of the current devolution policies, see Gold (1996) and Quigley and Rubinfeld (1996).

which equity problems emerging from Tiebout competition are serious enough to warrant some equity-enhancing intervention. This is most relevant to the provision of public education at the local level, where substantial intercommunity differences in wealth give rise to unfortunate inequalities in the provision of quality public schools across communities. In the absence of vouchers, which provide additional opportunities to residents in lower-income communities, the concern over such inequalities in public education funding has led to many different types of state interventions, ranging from foundation aid to equalization aid to centralization of all funding decisions. The California experience over the past twenty-five years has demonstrated that centralization is not the answer (in great part because too much local autonomy is lost in the process). This leaves states to choose between *equalizing aid,* under which the size of a school district's grant is inversely related to its property wealth (and which generally comes in matching-grant form), and *foundation aid,* which provides a lump sum amount of per-pupil spending to all or a selected number of needy districts and then allows districts to supplement this amount through local tax revenues.

Equalization aid, however, has the unfortunate tendency to introduce somewhat perverse incentives at the local level, as it, in essence, rewards local governments who fail to pursue policies that enhance local property values.[50] For this reason, we are most inclined to endorse the concept of limited foundation aid to selected school districts by state governments. Although this will not lead to equality of spending across districts (unless aid levels are extraordinarily high, causing no local government to supplement it), it does provide a minimum spending guarantee even in the poorest districts while, under sufficient insti-

---

50. In general, policies that enhance local property values are efficiency enhancing (Scotchmer 1994), and incentives that discourage local property value maximization may therefore be quite unhealthy. In the extreme, this can lead to perverse NIMBY policies in which local governments create adverse incentives for business formation in order to keep state aid levels high.

tutional restraints on state governments and under a sufficiently limited grant system, retaining a large measure of local autonomy (especially when foundation aid is only applicable to a small fraction of districts).

Throughout, however, we suggest that much of the economic benefit of federal systems must be embedded in the early design stages because political pressures and incentives created by the presence of monetary institutions encourage undue encroachment by the central government unless restraining political institutions are in place. In the United States, such institutions are not yet firmly established, causing concern over the evolution of currently developing block grant programs. These programs, while potentially healthy as a transitional device, may also represent the beginning of a slow collapse of the relatively successful U.S. federal system into a unitary state if they themselves become institutionalized. The appropriate design of the system must therefore take into account not only the standard public finance arguments but further considerations introduced by public choice theory as well as monetary theory.

References

Aaron, H., and W. Gale, eds. 1996 *Economic Effects of Fundamental Tax Reform*. Washington, D.C.: Brookings Institution.

Advisory Commission on Intergovernmental Relations. 1994. *Significant Features of Fiscal Federalism*. Washington D.C.: U.S. Government Printing Office.

Arnott, R., and R. Grieson. 1981. "Optimal Fiscal Policy for a State or Local Government." *Journal of Urban Economics* 9: 23–48.

Baron, D., and J. Ferejohn. 1989. "Bargaining Legislatures." *American Political Science Review* 83: 1182–206.

Bayoumi, T., and B. Eichengreen. 1994. "The Political Economy of Fiscal Restrictions: Implications for Europe from the United States." *European Economic Review* 38: 783–91.

Besharov, G., and A. Zweiman. 1997. "Increasing Returns in Production and Spill-over Effects of Regulation." Mimeo, Stanford University.

Boadway, R., and F. Flatters. 1982. "Efficiency and Equalization Payments in a Federal System of Government: A Synthesis and Extension of Recent Results." *Canadian Journal of Economics* 15: 613–33.

Boskin, M., ed. 1996. *Frontiers of Tax Reform.* Stanford: Hoover Institution Press.

Brennan, G., and J. Buchanan. 1977. "Towards a Tax Constitution for Leviathan." *Journal of Public Economics* 8: 255–73.

Courchene, T. 1994. *Social Canada in the Millennium: Reforming Imperatives and Restructuring Principles.* Toronto, Canada: C. D. Howe Institute.

Craig, S., and R. Inman. 1985. "Education, Welfare and the 'New' Federalism." In *Studies in State and Local Public Finance,* ed. H. Rosen. Chicago: University of Chicago Press.

Eberts, R., and T. Gronberg. 1988. "Can Competition among Local Governments Constrain Government Spending?" *Economic Review* (Federal Reserve Bank of Cleveland) 24: 2–9.

Epple, D., and T. Romer. 1991. "Mobility and Redistribution." *Journal of Political Economy* 99: 828–76.

Epple, D., and A. Zelenitz. 1981. "The Implications of Competition among Jurisdictions: Does Tiebout Need Politics?" *Journal of Economic Theory* 89: 1197–217.

Feldstein, M. 1975. "Wealth Neutrality and Local Choice in Public Education." *American Economic Review* 65: 75–89.

Feldstein, M., and M. Vaillant. 1994. "Can State Taxes Redistribute Income?" National Bureau of Economic Research (NBER) working paper no. 4785.

Fischel, W. 1992. "Property Taxation and the Tiebout Model: Evidence for the Benefit View versus the New View." *Journal of Economic Literature* 30: 171–77.

Fischer, R. 1996. *State and Local Public Finance.* Chicago: Irwin.

Frey, B., and R. Eichenberg. 1996. "To Harmonize or to Compete? That's Not the Question." *Journal of Public Economics* 60: 335–49.

Gold, S. 1996. "Issues Raised by the New Federalism." *National Tax Journal* 49: 273–87.

Gordon, R. 1983. "An Optimal Taxation Approach to Fiscal Federalism." *Quarterly Journal of Economics* 95: 567–86.

———. 1992. "Can Capital Income Taxes Survive in Open Economies?" *Journal of Finance* 47: 1159–80.

Gramlich, E. 1987. "Subnational Fiscal Policy." *Perspectives on Local Public Finance and Public Policy* 3: 3–27.

Gramlich, E., and D. Rubinfeld. 1982. "Micro Estimates of Public Spending Demand Functions and Tests of the Tiebout and Median Voter Hypotheses." *Journal of Political Economy* 90: 536–60.

Grieson, R. 1980. "Theoretical Analysis and Empirical Measurement of the Effects of the Philadelphia Income Tax." *Journal of Urban Economics* 8: 123–37.

Hall, R., and A. Rabushka. 1995. *The Flat Tax*. Stanford: Hoover Institution Press.

Hamilton, B. 1975. "Zoning and Property Taxes in a System of Local Governments." *Urban Studies* 12: 205–11.

———. 1976. "Capitalization of Interjurisdictional Differences in Local Tax Prices." *American Economic Review* 66: 743–53.

Hayek, F. A. 1945. "The Use of Knowledge in Society." *American Economic Review* 35: 519–30.

Hines, J., and R. Thaler. 1996. "The Flypaper Effect." *Journal of Economic Perspectives* 9: 217–26.

Hoxby, C. 1994. "Does Competition among Public Schools Benefit Students and Taxpayers? Evidence from Natural Variation in School Districting." NBER working paper no. 4979.

———. 1995. "Is There an Equity-Efficiency Trade-Off in School Finance? Tiebout and a Theory of the Local Public Good Producer." NBER working paper no. 5265.

———. 1997. "All School Finance Equalizations Are Not Created Equal: Marginal Tax Rates Matter." Mimeo, Harvard University.

Inman, R. 1988a. "Markets, Governments, and the 'New' Political Economy." In *Handbook of Public Economics*. Vol. 2, ed. A. Auerbach and M. Feldstein. Amsterdam: North Holland.

———. 1988b. "Federal Assistance and Local Services in the United States: The Evolution of a New Federalist Fiscal Order." In *Fiscal Federalism*, ed. H. Rosen. Chicago: University of Chicago Press.

Inman, R., and D. Rubinfeld. 1996. "Designing Tax Policy in Federalist Economies: An Overview." *Journal of Public Economics* 60: 307–34.

International Monetary Fund. 1996. *World Economic Outlook*, May.

Jones, R., and J. Whalley. 1988. "Regional Effects of Taxes in Canada: An Applied General Equilibrium Approach." *Journal of Public Economics* 37: 1–28.

Kimbell, L., and G. Harrison. 1984. "General Equilibrium Analysis of Regional Fiscal Incidence." In *Applied General Equilibrium Analysis*, ed. H. Scarf and J. Shoven. New York: Cambridge University Press.

Kolstad, C., and F. Wolak. 1983. "Competition in Interregional Taxation: The Case of Western Coal." *Journal of Political Economy* 91: 443–60.

———. 1985. "Strategy and Market Structure in Western Coal Taxation." *Review of Economics and Statistics* 67: 239–49.

Landsburg, S. 1995. *Price Theory and Applications*. Saint Paul, Minn.: Dryden Press.

Marlow, M. 1988. "Fiscal Decentralization and Government Size." *Public Choice* 56: 159–69.

McKinnon, R. 1994. "A Common Monetary Standard or a Common Currency for Europe?" *Scottish Journal of Political Economy* 41: 337–57.

———. 1995. "Intergovernmental Competition in Europe with and without a Common Currency." *Journal of Economic Policy Modeling*, pp. 463–78.

———. 1996a. *The Rules of the Game: International Money and Exchange Rates*. Cambridge, Mass.: MIT Press.

———. 1996b. "Monetary Regimes, Government Borrowing Constraints, and Market-Preserving Federalism: Implications for EMU." Paper presented at the Queens University conference on "The Nation State in a Global Information Era," with a comment by C. Ragan.

———. 1997. "Market Preserving Federalism in the American Monetary Union." In *Macroeconomic Dimensions of Public Finance: Essays in Honour of Vito Tanzi*, ed. M. Blejer and T. Ter-Minassian. London: Routledge.

McLure, C. 1975. "Integration of the Personal and Corporate Income Taxes: The Missing Element in Rent Tax Reform Proposals." *Harvard Law Review* 88: 532–82.

———. 1980. "The State Corporate Income Tax: Lambs in Wolves' Clothing." In *The Economics of Taxation*, ed. H. Aaron and M. Boskin. Washington, D.C.: Brookings Institution.

———. 1986. "Tax Competition: Is What's Good for the Private Goose Also Good for the Public Gander?" *National Tax Journal* 39: 341–48.

McLure, C., and P. Mieszkowski. 1983. *Fiscal Federalism and the Taxation of Natural Resources*. Lexington, Mass.: Lexington Books.

Mieszkowski, P. 1972. "The Property Tax: An Excise Tax or a Profits Tax?" *Journal of Public Economics* 1: 73–96.

Mieszkowski, P., and G. Zodrow. 1989. "Taxation and the Tiebout Model." *Journal of Economic Literature* 27: 1098–146.

Mintz, J., and H. Tulkens. 1996. "Optimality Properties of Alternative Systems of Taxation of Foreign Capital Income." *Journal of Public Economics* 60: 373–400.

Moffitt, R. 1984. "The Effects of Grants-in-Aid on State and Local Expenditures: The Case of AFDC." *Journal of Public Economics* 23: 279–305.

Morgan, J., W. Mutti, and M. Partridge. 1989. "A Regional General Equilibrium Model of the United States: Tax Effects on Factor Movements and Regional Production." *Review of Economics and Statistics* 71: 626–35.

Montinola, G., Y. Qian, and B. Weingast. 1994. "Federalism Chinese Style: The Political Basis for Economic Success in China." Mimeo, Stanford University.

Musgrave, R. A. 1959. *Theory of Public Finance: A Study in Public Economy.* New York: McGraw Hill.

Nechyba, T. 1996. "A Computable General Equilibrium Model of Intergovernmental Aid." *Journal of Public Economics* 62: 363–99.

———. 1997a. "Existence of Equilibrium and Stratification in Hierarchical and Local Public Goods Economies with Property Taxes and Voting." *Economic Theory*, forthcoming.

———. 1997b. "Local Property and State Income Taxes: The Role of Interjurisdictional Competition and Collusion." *Journal of Political Economy* 105: 351–84.

Nechyba, T., and R. Strauss. 1997. "Community Choice and Local Public Services: A Discrete Choice Approach." *Regional Science and Urban Economics*, forthcoming.

Niou, E., and P. Ordeshook. 1985. "Universalism in Congress." *American Journal of Political Science* 29: 246–59.

Niskanen, W. 1971. *Bureaucracy and Representative Government.* Chicago: Aldine-Atherton.

Oates, W. 1969. "The Effect of Property Taxes and Local Public Spending on Property Values: An Empirical Study of Tax Capitalization and the Tiebout Hypothesis." *Journal of Political Economy* 77: 757–71.

———. 1972. *Fiscal Federalism.* New York: Harcourt, Brace, Jovanovich.

———. 1985. "Searching for Leviathan: An Empirical Study." *American Economic Review* 75: 748–57.

———. 1989. "Searching for Leviathan: A Reply and Further Reflections." *American Economic Review* 79: 578–83.

———, ed. 1991. *Studies in Fiscal Federalism.* Worcester, Eng.: Billings & Sons Ltd.

Oates, W., and R. Schwab. 1988. "Economic Competition among Jurisdictions: Efficiency Enhancing or Distortion Inducing?" *Journal of Public Economics* 35: 333–53.

Organization for Economic Cooperation and Development (OECD). *World Economic Outlook.* Paris: OECD (various issues).

Papke, L. 1991. "Interstate Business Tax Differential and New Firm Location: Evidence from Panel Data." *Journal of Public Economics* 45: 47–68.

Pindyck, R. 1978. "Gains to Producers from the Cartelization of Exhaustible Resources." *Review of Economics and Statistics* 60: 238–51.

Quigley, J., and D. Rubinfeld. 1996. "Federalism and the Reductions in the Federal Budget." *National Tax Journal* 49: 289–302.

Riker, W. 1964. *Federalism: Origin, Operation and Significance.* Boston: Little Brown.

Rivlin, A. 1992. *Reviving the American Dream.* Washington, D.C.: Brookings Institution.

Rubinfeld, D. 1987. "The Economics of the Local Public Sector." In *Handbook of Public Economics.* Vol. 2, ed. A. Auerbach and M. Feldstein. Amsterdam: North Holland.

Sargent, T., and N. Wallace. 1981. "Some Unpleasant Monetarist Arithmetic." *Quarterly Review* (Federal Reserve Bank of Minneapolis) 5 (fall): 1–17.

Scotchmer, S. 1994. "Public Goods and the Invisible Hand." In *Modern Public Finance,* ed. J. Quigley and E. Smolenski. Cambridge, Mass.: Harvard University Press.

Shaviro, D. 1992. "An Economic and Political Look at Federalism in Taxation." *Michigan Law Review* 90: 895–991.

Shepsle, K. 1979. "Institutional Arrangements and Equilibrium in Multidimensional Voting Models." *American Journal of Political Science* 28: 27–59.

Shepsle, K., and B. Weingast. 1984. "Legislative Politics and Budget Outcomes." In *Federal Budget Policy in the 1980s,* ed. G. Mills and J. Palmer. Washington, D.C.: Urban Institute.

Starrett, D. 1980. "Measuring Externalities and Second Best Distortions in the Theory of Local Public Goods." *Econometrica* 48: 627–42.

Strauss, R. 1974. "The Impact of Block Grants on Local Expenditures and Property Tax Rates." *Journal of Public Economics,* pp. 269–84.

———. 1990. "Fiscal Federalism and the Changing Global Economy." *National Tax Journal* 43: 315–20.

Tiebout, C. 1956. "A Pure Theory of Local Expenditures." *Journal of Political Economy* 64: 416–24.

U.S. Department of Commerce, Bureau of the Census. 1991. *Geographic Mobility: March 1987 to March 1990*. Washington, D.C.: U.S. Government Printing Office.

Weingast, B. 1979. "A Rational Perspective on Congressional Norms." *American Journal of Political Science* 23: 245–62.

———. 1993. "Constitutions as Governance Structures: The Political Foundations of Secure Markets." *Journal of Institutional and Theoretical Economics* 149: 286–311.

———. 1995. "The Economic Role of Political Institutions: Market-Preserving Federalism and Economic Development." *Journal of Law, Economics, and Organization* 11: 1–31.

Weingast, B., K. Shepsle, and C. Johnson. 1981. "The Political Economy of Benefits and Costs: A Neoclassical Approach to Distributive Politics." *Journal of Political Economy* 89: 642–64.

Wildasin, D. 1986. *Urban Public Finance*. New York: Harwood Academic Publishers.

———. 1989. "Interjurisdictional Capital Mobility: Fiscal Externality and Corrective Subsidy." *Journal of Urban Economics* 25: 193–212.

———. 1997. "Factor Mobility and Redistributive Policy: Local and International Perspectives." In *Public Finance in a Changing World*, ed. P. Sorensen. New York: Macmillan.

Wilson, J. 1986. "A Theory of Inter-Regional Tax Competition." *Journal of Urban Economics* 19: 296–315.

Wyckoff, J. 1996. "To What Extent Is Education a Public Good?" In *Readings, Issues, and Problems in Public Finance*, ed. E. Brown and R. Moore. Chicago: Irwin.

Wyckoff, P. 1991. "The Elusive Flypaper Effect." *Journal of Urban Economics* 30: 310–28.

Zax, J. 1989. "Is there a Leviathan in Your Neighborhood?" *American Economic Review* 79: 560–67.

Zodrow, G., and P. Mieszkowski. 1986. "Pigou, Tiebout Property Taxation and the Underprovision of Local Public Goods." *Journal of Urban Economics* 19: 356–70.

PART TWO

Craig Volden

CHAPTER TWO

Entrusting the States with Welfare Reform

On August 22, 1996, President Bill Clinton signed the Personal Responsibility and Work Opportunity Reconciliation Act of 1996, ending six decades of federal entitlement to welfare benefits. This landmark legislation turned many welfare decisions over to the states through a system of block grants with few federal strings attached. Initiated by the Republican Congress in 1995 as part of the Contract with America, the reform had twice been vetoed by the president. The National Governors' Association breathed new life into the plan with its support in early 1996, such that, by the summer, welfare reform was as overwhelmingly supported in Congress and in state capitals as it was broadly popular with the American public. With regard to its policy implications, this reform raises the question Can the states be trusted to provide suitable levels of welfare benefits and to help individuals move from welfare to work?

The media, politicians, policy analysts, economists, and political scientists divide into two sides on the issue, often along partisan lines. Supporters of increased devolution of policy decisions to the states argue that the 1996 welfare reforms will give the states freedom to engage in policy experimentation and innovation without having to meet undue federal requirements. Further, competition between the states will lead states to act as "policy laboratories," each trying to find the best and most efficient ways of moving welfare recipients into the workplace. Opponents of increased federalism, however, argue that state competition will lead to a "race to the bottom" in welfare benefits. They claim that the new legislation grants states the *ability* to provide the lowest level of services that the public will allow; further, state governments will have the *incentives* to cut benefits lest their states become "welfare magnets," which attract potential recipients with relatively high levels of benefits.

It is too early in the reform process to determine the outcome of this transfer of power to the states. (States have until July 1, 1997, to convert to block grants and to submit a plan to the secretary of Health and Human Services, although many are making the switch earlier.) It is not too early, however, to clearly analyze the possibilities for policy innovations or benefit cuts in the states as a result of the 1996 reforms. In this chapter, I first explain how concerns about the role of the states in our federal system can be addressed through a focus on welfare and, in particular, on the Aid to Families with Dependent Children (AFDC) Program, now the Temporary Assistance for Needy Families Program. I then turn to the specific arguments about state prospects for experimentation and for benefit cuts, linking current decisions to earlier welfare policies. Finally, I address the effects of economic, political, and electoral constraints on state policymakers' decisions about welfare reforms, arguing that institutional structures as well as public preferences will limit the amount of change and innovation.

Although the current welfare reforms encourage revision of state policies, states have always had the ability to lower benefit levels and thus engage in a race to the bottom. Such a race has been limited or nonexistent thus far, constrained by the preferences of state populations and by the bureaucratic and political institutions surrounding welfare and maintaining base levels of benefits. The 1996 welfare reforms reflect public preferences for a shift of power to the states and for a fervent attempt to move welfare recipients into the workplace. But these preferences are not lacking in compassion for needy families, for hungry children, or for the temporarily unemployed. Whether at the state or the federal level, policymakers are responsive to voter preferences, meaning that we are not going to see immediate or dramatic cuts in welfare benefits in the states.

What we *are* likely to see, however, are attempts at policy innovations in the states aimed at providing jobs or job training to individual welfare recipients. The question then will be, How successful are states at moving recipients into the workplace? State governments will again be constrained by public preferences for spending on job-training programs, by the difficulties of working through public welfare bureaucracies, and by the political and economic limitations on reform proposals. Nevertheless, there are many reasons to believe that the states are better able to handle this transition to the workplace than the federal government. Although the states face tighter financial limits than the federal government, states and localities are closer to the people and thus have better access to information about the needs of recipients and about community employment opportunities. This information, along with increased incentives to move people off welfare, will provide the best possible environment for successful experimentation in welfare policy.

Temporary Assistance for Needy Families

The questions of a race to the bottom and of state innovations with regard to welfare policy must be addressed by focusing on the AFDC Program, now the Temporary Assistance for Needy Families Program. The other major welfare programs, including Food Stamps and Medicaid, either are entirely funded at the federal level or are so heavily regulated by the federal law that states have no freedom to vary benefit levels.[1]

The 1996 welfare reforms replaced AFDC with Temporary Assistance for Needy Families (TANF), which turned the matching-fund grants to the states into block grants.[2] This legislation brought about three main changes that are important to our understanding of the likely results of the current reforms: (1) restructuring the program funding, (2) limiting eligibility, and (3) imposing work requirements. The first change transformed the matching-fund grants of the AFDC program into block grants. Under the matching-fund provisions, state governments set benefit levels for families receiving aid and a portion of the cost was then paid by the federal government. In the poorest states (in terms of average income), the federal government paid up to 65 percent of the costs of the payments. In the wealthiest states, the federal government paid half the program's costs. If a state decided to increase monthly payments by a dollar, it paid only thirty-five to fifty cents of that dollar. Likewise, state savings from benefit cuts were limited to that same fraction of a dollar for every dollar cut.

With the transformation of the program to block grants to the states, this requirement of partial federal funding disappears. The federal government still pays for a portion of the program, but it now provides about the same-sized grant regardless of the level of benefits given by the states to welfare recipients. The block grants under the TANF Program provide a lump sum of money to each state each year that is expected to total about $16.4 billion annually through fiscal year

---

1. Although there were also some changes limiting Food Stamps and the Supplemental Security Income (SSI) Program, the reforms were mainly aimed at eliminating AFDC and establishing TANF. The initial Republican proposals had viewed welfare reform in its broadest sense, looking to give states more control with regard to Medicaid, Food Stamps, and school lunches, as well as AFDC. Only after Congress agreed to abandon these other changes—Medicaid reform in particular—did President Clinton end his opposition to the legislation.

2. For a summary of the final political decisions and the program provisions, see Katz (1996a, 1996b).

2001. The amount each state receives is based on the size of its grant from the federal government in 1995, 1994, or the average of 1992–94, whichever is higher. Once that amount is set, it will not increase or decrease over the next five years,[3] regardless of whether states increase or decrease their benefit levels or remove people from or add them to welfare.[4] This is a dramatic departure from the matching funds, which depended solely on the benefit levels and the number of recipients in each state.

The argument that state governments will now cut their benefit levels comes in part from the fact that now a cut of a dollar in monthly payments translates to a full dollar in savings to the states, whereas previously such a cut saved state governments only up to fifty cents. Whether such benefit reductions would be good or bad is a matter of opinion. Some students of federalism argue that intergovernmental grants provide an undue stimulus for spending by the recipient government. They believe that grants make the program seem less expensive, thus leading to overspending and a decline in accountability in that taxing and spending are no longer linked. Others argue that this stimulant effect is necessary to compensate for the natural reduction in benefits due to competition between states. They suggest that, out of fear of attracting other states' welfare recipients (or as an attempt to scare off their own), states will provide lower benefits out of a sense of competition than they would were they completely isolated. This leads these students of federalism to argue for grants that bring the spending levels back up or for national control of redistributive programs.

Regardless of which side makes the more persuasive case, it seems evident that the reforms will indeed provide state governments with

---

3. This constant funding means that the amounts will decline in real terms because of inflation. This accounts for part of the federal savings from welfare reform, with much of the rest of the savings coming from denying benefits to immigrants.

4. This is true, of course, only within some broad range. As detailed elsewhere in the chapter, states must maintain certain spending levels and can receive additional federal rainy-day funding if they face particularly difficult times.

increased incentives for benefit cuts. But these are not incentives that have been unknown to governors and state legislators. States have always had the ability to save funds by reducing welfare benefits. The question is, What causes particular welfare levels in particular states?

Certainly states have a difficult time maintaining high benefit levels during periods of population growth (when part of that growth also means expanding welfare rolls), during periods of high unemployment, and during economic recessions. Thus in the 1996 act the federal government set aside additional funds that would be available under each of these possibilities: $800 million for states with growing populations, $2 billion for states with high unemployment, and $1.7 billion in loans available during economic downturns. The law also provides financial incentives for states that best move recipients into the workplace and for states that reduce out-of-wedlock births. Other funding issues of note are that states must continue to spend at least 75 percent of the amount of state funds that they had been spending on welfare before the reforms and that states may provide newcomers from another state the same level of benefits they would have received in their former state for up to one year. These provisions discourage dramatic benefit cuts, as well as one of the claimed "needs" for dramatic cuts (to avoid becoming a welfare magnet).

The second major change brought about by the 1996 welfare reforms limits the eligibility of welfare recipients. The law mandates that the federal block grant funds cannot be used to provide welfare benefits to adults who have received welfare for more than five years in their lifetime. Likewise, states cannot use federal funds to provide benefits to those adults who have not begun working after two years on welfare. This means, among other things, that the broad *entitlement*—providing payments or services to all those who fall in a particular group—to welfare has ended. As the size of many entitled groups can grow dramatically over time, federal entitlements are of great concern to those interested in limiting federal spending. Never before has Congress ended a major federal entitlement or transformed one into block grants to the states. Indeed, limiting spending was one of the motivations behind the switch to block grants and the eligibility limits on welfare recipients.

States can enact additional restrictions and exemptions on eligibility. For example, the federal government has mandated that no convicted drug felons receive benefits, but states could opt out of this provision. States could also deny benefits to unwed parents under the age of eighteen who do not live with an adult and attend school; states could refuse payments to noncitizen legal immigrants; and they could deny additional benefits to mothers who have children while receiving welfare. The last of these possibilities, known as the *family cap*, is likely to be hotly contested in statehouses across the nation. At issue is how to continue aid to newborn children without encouraging welfare mothers to have additional children.

The third major change brought about by the welfare reform package concerns work requirements. As mentioned above, adult recipients will now be required to begin working within two years of receiving benefits. The law also provides states with incentives to help their recipients find jobs. As of 1997, states are required to have 25 percent of their welfare caseload participating in "work activities," ranging from job skills training to unsubsidized employment, for at least twenty hours a week. The percentage of the caseload involved and the amount of work required increases every year, such that, by the year 2002, 50 percent of welfare recipients will need to be participating in work-related activities for at least thirty hours a week. States that fail to reach these levels will receive lower federal grants; those that best achieve the welfare-to-work transition will be rewarded financially.

Hopes and Fears of Welfare Reform

Opponents of the block grant approach to welfare argue that competition among states will lead to a race to the bottom in welfare services.

In the other chapters of this volume, the values of competition come through clearly. In the realm of welfare policy, however, there is the fear that competition will lead to *less-favorable* policy outcomes than those that would occur without such competition. The basis for this fear is found in an understanding of how state competition works in a federal system.

The recent debate surrounding welfare has taken a form familiar to students of U.S. federalism. The underlying questions concern which level of government should be entrusted with what programs using what tax bases. Of course, different people give different answers to these questions. In one view, governance should be as close to the people as possible. Whatever can be left to the people should be, without government involvement. Whatever cannot be left to the people themselves should be handled at the local level. That which cannot be handled locally should be done by the state, and that which the state cannot do is left to the national government. This line of reasoning often leaves the federal government with little beyond national defense. It also raises some questions. For example, although pollution *could* be controlled locally or by the states, when it crosses these boundaries do we not need federal government involvement?

A second view is that the level of government that can best, or most efficiently, govern should be entrusted to do so. State and local governments often have better access to information and to the demands of the public and are thus in a better position to make laws and regulations than is the one-size-fits-all federal government. Competition between the states and localities leads to more efficient policies and resource usage than a single national decision would produce.[5] Large projects or those that do not benefit from state-to-state variation, however, might be better handled by the federal government. Those who espouse this view argue that national defense, redistribution programs,

---

5. This argument has arisen out of the work of Charles Tiebout (1956), which has been questioned as much for its assumptions as for its conclusions.

Social Security, and the like can be more efficiently handled by the federal government than by fifty bureaucracies.[6] In such a case, state governments would either be redundant or would face incentives to skimp on services, hoping that surrounding states would pick up the slack and the tab.

Two main supporters of this view are Paul Peterson and Mark Rom. In their 1990 book, *Welfare Magnets*, they argue that state competition leads to low levels of welfare benefits. States that provide high benefit levels retain their welfare recipients and attract recipients from surrounding states who move because of the prospect of larger payments. In a related argument, *taxpayers* may leave a state with high benefit levels (and thus high taxes) to find states more in line with their preferences. Afraid of becoming welfare magnets, states that give high service levels face incentives to cut back on their welfare payments or be overrun by a deluge of poor people seeking benefits. Peterson and Rom argue that this fear will lead one state after another to cut their benefit levels in a race to the bottom.

Although this argument has some merit, the evidence is that welfare magnets seem only weakly attractive. For example, a study by Hanson and Hartman (1994) finds, first, that disadvantaged individuals do not move from one state to another to receive higher benefit levels and, second, that poor people hardly move from state to state for any reason. Hanson and Hartman argue that the number of families and individuals who move is so small as to have little impact on state welfare expenditures. Even Peterson and Rom have recently come to recognize that "there is at most only modest evidence" in support of some of their claims and that the most generous states appear to be "only moderately magnetic" (Peterson et al. 1996, 3). Nevertheless, they still contend that the *fear* of becoming welfare magnets keeps the eyes of

---

6. Paul Peterson (1995) specifies this "functional federalism" in more detail, contrasting that argument nicely with what he calls "legislative federalism."

state governors firmly fixed on the other states, in what could result in a race to the bottom.

With regard to the welfare reforms of 1996, forms of this argument have arisen in the media and in policy circles. For example, Robert Greenstein, executive director of the liberal Center on Budget and Policy Priorities, said, "I don't think it's possible to design a block grant to provide what I would regard as adequate protection . . . and [that] does not substantially increase the risk of a race to the bottom" (*Congressional Quarterly Weekly Report* 1996, 1028). The argument in its most basic form is that, now that the states have control of welfare, they are in a position to cut benefits to their lowest levels.[7]

In actuality states have *always* had the ability (and those types of incentives) to cut welfare benefits. Since the inception of the Aid to Dependent Children Program in 1935, governors and state legislatures have had the power to set the level of benefits in their states. The only difference between the matching grants and the block grants in this regard is what fraction of the payments (and changes in payments) would be paid for by the federal government. So if there were to be such a race to the bottom with regard to AFDC, it would likely have already occurred.

But no such race has taken place. Consider, for example, average monthly payments to welfare recipients in the fifty states during the 1970s and 1980s. During these two decades many critics feared cuts. In the 1970s, with the rise of the Food Stamps Program, states faced incentives to reduce AFDC benefits in order to increase the payments they would receive from the federal government through Food Stamps

---

7. The next iteration of this argument is expected to be that states that are the most successful in their welfare-to-work programs will become welfare-to-work magnets, attracting people who want to participate in these programs and find jobs. Although this effect is again expected to be limited, at least it is in the positive direction of people who want jobs moving to where job opportunities are available. It is unlikely that such pressures would cause state governments to try to make ineffective programs out of a fear of attracting new recipients if their programs are successful.

given to welfare recipients. Because the federal government picked up the full cost of Food Stamps and only part of the AFDC costs, states had the incentive to cut welfare benefits. Likewise, in the 1980s, states and localities were expected to respond to the larger burden of payments due to declining federal grants by cutting back state and local programs, including aid to the poor. Each of these conditions and incentives to cut benefits could have set off a race to the bottom, according to those who fear leaving welfare reform to the states.

But the evidence suggests that very few states made sizable welfare cuts. Figure 1 details the year-in and year-out changes in average benefit levels in the states through these two decades. Fifty states over twenty years yields one thousand chances to jump out of the starting blocks in the race to the bottom. But in only fifteen cases did states cut the nominal average monthly benefit by 5 percent or more from one year to the next. In only five cases were the cuts as great as 10 percent. Further, even these cases were more like foot faults than the start of a race: in all five instances of noticeable benefit cuts, the states restored the benefit levels within two or three years, often with very sizable benefit increases.

Most states' average benefit levels from one year to the next are stable, perhaps increasing slightly in terms of current dollar expenditures, with about three-quarters of the data between a 5 percent decline in payment levels and a 10 percent increase (see figure 1). In six out of every seven year-to-year intervals, average welfare payments were higher from one year to the next.

This does not mean that welfare benefits have been increasing or even maintaining their value over time. Indeed, in real terms, benefit levels have been declining somewhat. Governors and state legislators have been letting inflation do their dirty work for them, simply not adjusting benefits upward enough to make up for the reduced purchasing power of inflation-decayed welfare benefits. For those concerned with declining benefits, this was much more of a problem during the inflationary 1970s than it is today. And, in terms of a race, this is more

Figure 1   State Changes in Welfare Benefits, 1970s and 1980s

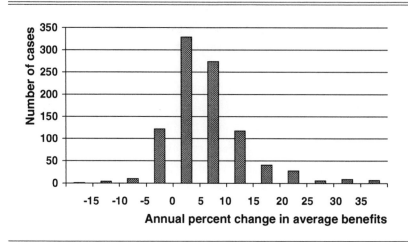

like a common drift, keeping all the states in similar proportions to one another. The most generous states have continued to pay three to five times the benefit levels of the poorest states.

As of the mid-1990s, about five million families were receiving AFDC payments. The average family on welfare received about $375 a month in AFDC benefits, for a total program cost of nearly $23 billion annually. Families in the states of Alaska, California, Connecticut, Hawaii, Massachusetts, Minnesota, New York, Rhode Island, and Vermont on average received more than $500 per month; families in Alabama, Arkansas, Louisiana, Mississippi, South Carolina, Tennessee, and Texas received less than $200 per month. These state differences are due to a variety of factors including preferences and ideology of the state populations, fiscal constraints on the state governments, and cost of living in the various states.[8]

---

8. For recent evidence of wealthier states providing higher levels of support to the disadvantaged than poorer states, see Brown (1995), Dye (1990), Plotnick and Winters

These crude figures indicate that, despite possible incentives of the high-benefit states to cut their payments, many of the wealthiest states still provide several times the benefits of the poorest states. The paucity of evidence of the disadvantaged streaming from one state to another may be due to a variety of factors. First, AFDC payments are just one of the benefits these individuals are able to receive as assistance. The Food Stamps Program alone reduces the cross-state variance in welfare payments by about half. In a study of interstate equity of payments, Robert Albritton (1989) finds that states with higher-than-average incomes provide higher benefit levels but that any such correlation vanishes once Food Stamps are included in the calculation. Second, although the benefit levels might be higher in another state, so too would the costs of living, making the move unattractive for many.

Finally, there are large costs to moving from one state to another (whether financial, social, or otherwise). Welfare recipients would have to envision many years of benefits to make up for the costs of the move. Before 1969, a number of states denied welfare benefits to those who had not resided in the state for at least one year. In that year, in *Shapiro v. Thompson*, the Supreme Court ruled that New York's requirement of this nature violated equal protection under the Fourteenth Amendment. Peterson and Rom argue that this restriction stopped the type of migration between states that they had expected to see following the repeal of these various laws after the Court's ruling. In a similar vein, two provisions of the 1996 welfare reform legislation make movement from one state to another *less attractive* to welfare recipients. First, the bill allows states to give the same level of payments to newcomers to the state that they were receiving in their previous home states for up to one year, eliminating the immediate advantage

---

(1985), and Tweedie (1994). With respect to political or partisan characteristics influencing policy, see especially Brown (1995) and Plotnick and Winters (1985).

of moving to a more generous state. Additionally, the legislation also dramatically reduces the long-term advantage of such a move. With the restriction on lifetime benefits to five years, and the need to move from welfare to work within two years of first receiving welfare, recipients no longer face the multiple years of benefit increases that could come in a move from one state to the next.

As a result, the current welfare reforms should serve to *reduce* state officials' fears of their state becoming a welfare magnet if they continue to provide high levels of benefits. Because the idea of a race to the bottom in benefits is often linked to this fear, supporters of this argument should be relieved that the incentives for such benefit cuts have been diminished.

Innovation and Experimentation in the States

Just as opponents of the devolution in welfare policy to the various states tend to raise one prevalent argument—that states would cut benefit levels dramatically—so do supporters of the change come back to one argument. Those supporting the transfer of power to the states emphasize the idea of state experimentation and innovation. This argument, like that of a race to the bottom, has its roots in competition between the states. Because states are constantly striving to provide more-attractive policies than their surrounding states to lure businesses and maintain their tax bases, among other things, they seek out innovative and efficient ways to perform the various functions of government. Of course, even without the added incentives of competition with other states, politicians within each state attempt to enact policies that are politically beneficial. Often this involves policy changes that could serve as useful examples for the other states.

This concept of states as "laboratories of democracy" was articulated by Justice Louis Brandeis in 1932, when he wrote

> There must be power in the States and the Nation to remould, through experimentation, our economic practices and institutions to meet changing social and economic needs. . . . Denial of the right to experiment may be fraught with serious consequences to the Nation. It is one of the happy incidents of the federal system that a single courageous State may, if its citizens choose, serve as a laboratory; and try novel social and economic experiments without risk to the rest of the country. (Osborne, 1988)

Central to this idea of policy experimentation is the belief that other states, or the nation as a whole, may benefit from the "novel experiments" in a handful of states. Policymakers in one state can assess and avoid the experiments that fail elsewhere, and they can admire and attempt on their own those that are successful.

With regard to welfare reform, states are beginning to experiment with moving welfare recipients into the workplace. The welfare reform law requires state governments to meet various federal employment standards, and it provides state policymakers with incentives to move their recipients off welfare in order to reap budget savings from fewer families receiving state aid. Although it is true that states had some of these incentives under the AFDC program, the benefits of moving recipients into the workplace were limited by the matching form of the federal grant. Indeed, just as the opponents of block grants argue that there are now added incentives to cut back on benefits, so too should supporters argue that there are now incentives to move people from welfare to work. Previous state spending on welfare-to-work programs that brought about lower AFDC rolls would have resulted in state savings of less than fifty cents on the dollar, as fewer recipients meant lower federal grants. Furthermore, the poorer states, perhaps those most in need of moving their populations into the workplace, faced the smallest incentives to do so, as they had the highest federal matching rates and thus would reap the smallest savings from moving their recipients off welfare.

As such, under the old system, even if state-run welfare-to-work programs would be cost-effective, state governments would not attempt them. If a state could spend less than a dollar on worker training (or on other work-related programs) for every dollar saved in reduced welfare payments, a good case could be made for government involvement. But when the federal government claims fifty to sixty-five cents of that saved dollar through a decrease in the grant to the state, states attempt only extremely cost-effective programs. This is not to say that governments base their policies solely on their cost-effectiveness. But many states could not attempt worthwhile programs to move people from welfare to work because of budget considerations and the reduction in AFDC grants that would accompany the move off welfare. Now, with the block grant system, states can keep any money that they are able to save through reducing the welfare rolls and use these funds, perhaps, on further welfare-to-work programs. No longer is it the case that the federal government will "reward" the states that help people move off welfare by cutting the federal grant.

The switch from matching-fund grants to block grants, along with the added incentives of the new law, should open the floodgates for experimentation in the states in welfare-to-work programs. Some states that already meet the federal standards of a certain percentage of their recipients being involved in work-related activities have the luxury either of being able to sit back and view experiments in the other states or of being able to attempt bold new programs that may indeed fail but could also bring sizable rewards. Other states, facing the urgent struggle of meeting the federal standards, are being forced into their policy laboratories immediately.

States will attempt a broad range of experimental programs. Perhaps the threat of losing their assistance within two years will lead the disadvantaged individuals on welfare into more zealous searches for unsubsidized employment. It is unlikely, however, that many states will rely on this option alone. Nor are they likely to rely on the goodwill of corporations to hire a million welfare recipients, as was being suggested by President Clinton early in 1997. States could provide temporary subsidies for public- or private-sector employment. They could help fund on-the-job, vocational-educational, and jobs skills training. States could encourage young recipients to continue to attend secondary schools or to receive a high school equivalency degree. And they could assist recipients in their job searches through a variety of means. Each of these programs has a cost and limitations on its likelihood of success. Depending on how these programs are structured, on whether and where jobs are available, on the skills needed by the workforce, and on many other factors, some experiments will be successes and others will be failures. This is always the case.

The question is, In addition to states and localities learning *over time*, can they learn *from one another?* In other words, can states function as policy laboratories? The evidence from other policy arenas has been mixed. With regard to states discovering policies that then are adopted and work well at the national level, scholars have been rightly skeptical. Because of the different nature of politics, economic conditions, population diversity, scale, and many other factors, policy successes in the states may not lead to policy successes nationally. It should not be a surprise that a health care system that works well in Hawaii might not appeal to the American public as a whole. Keith Boeckelman's (1992) survey of major federal and state policy adoptions shows not only that there is limited success in state programs subsequently adopted at the federal level but also that the federal government is about as likely to adopt programs that failed in the states as it is to adopt state policy successes. David Osborne (1988) looks at state economic and education policies that could perhaps serve as models for federal activities. He highlights politicians and policies in the states that he believes would well serve the nation as a whole. One interesting prediction that he makes is that the policies and persona of then Arkansas governor Bill Clinton could provide a model for successful policies and politicians nationwide. Indeed, many of the proposals and decisions that Clinton has made with mixed success in Washington have mirrored what he successfully attempted in Arkansas. It is perhaps easier to carry plans from state to state than from a state to Washington.

The use of experiments in one state as blueprints for policies in another has been studied in terms of the "diffusion" of policies from one state to the next.[9] Several conditions need to be met for innovations in one place to be adopted elsewhere. Governors and state legislators must be aware of the experimental design in other states through policy studies, media exposure, or personal contacts with policymakers in other states, "taking cues" from sources external to their own states (Freeman 1985). With regard to each policy arena, some states are viewed as "policy leaders," those that surrounding states look to for policy innovation (Lutz 1987). States may take the leadership role because they are in a financial position to attempt significant change, because they are forced into extreme experimentation by desperate times, or because governors or others are looking for broad media attention to advance their political careers.

Kollman, Miller, and Page (1995) take a theoretical approach to the issue of states as policy laboratories. They demonstrate, among other things, that, as states find themselves with increasingly different policy objectives from those of their neighbors, the usefulness of policy laboratories declines. Likewise, the benefits of experimentation depend on the search mechanisms to find beneficial policies and on whether each state would choose immediately to follow the successes of other states.

In a broader sense, the usefulness of states as policy laboratories depends on a variety of factors. Policymakers in states that have general similarities can benefit greatly from seeing the results of innovative attempts. And yet, just as conducting the same scientific experiment over and over again may lead to less scientific progress than testing a

---

9. See Freeman (1985), Gray (1973), Lutz (1987), Savage (1985), and Walker (1969).

variety of theories, so too does diversity in states' experimentation help bring about greater policy advances (see table 1).

Similarity in policy objectives and abilities is essential to gaining significant benefits from experimentation across states. Clearly, if one state is trying to reform welfare and another is intent on altering its criminal justice system, there would be little or no overlap in the policy ideas that flow from these very differently aimed experiments. But if every state is intent on welfare reform, the flow of ideas and stories of policy successes among the states would be high. Although it is necessary to have similar goals and policy objectives, it is just as necessary to have similar abilities across states. Political conditions vary dramatically from one state to the next, from the professionalization, goals, and aspirations of state legislatures to the political leanings of governors to the role of interest groups to the delegation of powers to bureaucracies to the ideological stance of the population as a whole. Similarities along these dimensions, as well as in states' economic abilities, provide the basis for policy triumphs from one state to be successfully adopted in another. As the economic conditions or political constraints vary, even the best of policies in one state may have no chance of survival elsewhere.

Although similarities in state goals and abilities are crucial to the success of policy laboratories, we must also focus on the similarities

Table 1   Benefits from States as Policy Laboratories

		Similarities across States in Goals, Abilities	
		Similar	*Different*
Similarities of experimentation	*Similar*	Moderate benefits	Low benefits
	Different	High benefits	Limited benefits

and differences between the types of experiments attempted from state to state. If all the states approached the task of moving welfare recipients into the workplace through the same types of programs, say, subsidized private-sector employment, we might indeed learn about the best mechanisms, incentives, and characteristics to make such a program work. But we would know little about whether that method is more cost-effective or more beneficial than intensive job skills training, promotion of secondary school education, vocational education, subsidization in the public sector, or the various other program types. As such, diversity in the area of policy experimentation is essential for achieving the greatest benefits from using states as policy laboratories.

As indicated in the upper-left box in table 1, similarities in the goals and abilities of states, combined with similar experiments across states, will produce moderate benefits in terms of diffusion and value of successful policies. The highest benefits of policy experimentation are likely to come when states have similar goals and abilities but initially attempt very different policy changes, as noted in the lower-left box in the table. The attempts at different policies in the various states mean that a broad range of policy options is being considered. The similarities in objectives and abilities in the various states mean that a policy success in one state can easily be adopted in another state.

In the right half of table 1, states become less useful as policy laboratories.[10] When states pursue different goals or face remarkably different political constraints and economic limitations, they cannot easily adopt an experiment from another state. Similar experiments in states with different goals and abilities are not only of low benefit to those states but are also unlikely to occur. The diversity of interests,

---

10. One thing to note is that there are no necessary cutoffs between the boxes in the table. Rather, the benefits exist in a continuum across these dimensions. Clearly no two states are identical in their preferences, institutions, and policy objectives. Nor are they necessarily all that dissimilar, as all states are basically trying to provide policies that reflect the preferences of their present or desired populations of residents, businesses, and interests.

objectives, and abilities would likely bring about different policies and experiments in decidedly different states. The final quadrant of table 1 is where states with different goals and abilities adopt different types of policies. Here again the benefits of states as policy laboratories are limited but still may be present, telling policymakers what works and what doesn't across a broad range of conditions and policies.[11]

With regard to state-to-state comparisons over welfare reform, we are likely to see moderate to high benefits from using states as policy laboratories. All the states face similar goals and objectives. Although the states are diverse in their economic abilities and political objectives, the continued existence of the federal grants will provide some of the initial funding necessary to attempt welfare-to-work programs.[12] With regard to the types of experimentation across the states, it is already clear that there will be significant variation in state plans. States such as California are considering tightening the federal standards to require that recipients begin work within one year of receiving benefits, while other states are exploring the possibility of spending their own funds to continue to support the disadvantaged beyond the federal deadlines. Some plans place a greater emphasis on individuals finding their own way, while others provide more job training and job placement. Wisconsin, for example, encourages individual effort by requiring potential recipients to engage in sixty hours of job search activities before being eligible for welfare payments. The New Jersey plan focuses on child care, providing subsidies for parents' child care needs

---

11. This description need not be limited to state-to-state policy comparisons. States may also serve as laboratories for federal policies. Here table 1 demonstrates the limitations on federal policy successes that come from the states. Politically, conditions vary dramatically between state governments and the federal government. Different interest groups are dominant; different institutional structures play a role; politicians have different aspirations. Economically and demographically, the federal government is also so dramatically different from the states that policy successes or failures in the states may have little to do with their chances once adopted by the federal government.

12. An additional funding advantage for the states has come through the decline in welfare rolls over the past two years owing to an economic recovery.

while they are at work. New Jersey will also ease the transition to the workplace through vouchers for transportation, job training, and job placement. Some states, such as Texas, are hoping to take the vouchers idea further, into the realm of privatization of many welfare services. Other states are pushing the idea of policy laboratories an additional step further, giving localities a more sizable role in the reforms. Governor George Pataki's plan in New York calls for block grants to local governments, in the hope that municipalities will find the best programs through local innovation. In contrast, New Jersey has considered limiting or eliminating a number of municipal welfare offices.

This broad range of alternatives and similarity of purposes indicates that, in the case of welfare reform, states may indeed serve as policy laboratories. Regardless of their role as laboratories, or their incentives for competition with one another, the states may be better able to handle this transition from welfare to work than would the federal government. It is at the state and local levels, closest to the people, that information is most readily available on job prospects, on the types of training and incentives needed to match the unemployed with sufficiently high-paying jobs to support their families, and on the constraints on welfare recipients in their attempts to move smoothly into the workforce. Only by addressing many of these underlying problems will states reach solutions; indeed, these solutions may vary from state to state and community to community.

Meeting Public Opinion

The previous two sections suggest two conclusions. First, we are unlikely to see a race to the bottom in welfare benefits; second, the states may serve us well as laboratories of democracy for welfare reform. This leads to the questions of *why* we have not yet seen dramatic state cuts in welfare and of *how great* the policy innovations will be. Two main factors limit both benefit cuts and the possibilities of success in state reforms: (1) the general will of the public within states and (2) the bureaucratic and political institutions constraining policy change and innovation. It is to the first of these that I turn.

As argued above, competition between states could place pressures on the states to provide lower welfare benefits, or competition could place the states in a position of fighting for the best incentives and programs to move recipients into the workplace. But, as Thomas Dye (1990, 189) argues, the competition between states actually serves the larger purpose of encouraging state legislators and governors to better represent public preferences:

> Competition encourages policy responsiveness. Welfare policies, like all other policies, are more responsive to citizen demands when undertaken by multiple competitive governments rather than monopoly government. The effect of competition is neither to lower nor to raise welfare spending but to bring it in line with citizen demands. Competitive governments must seek to match their welfare policies with both the compassion and the prudence of their citizens.

The question we may then ask is, What are citizens' demands regarding welfare reform? Recently compiled surveys show some surprising results and indicate that in many ways the 1996 welfare reform legislation and the subsequent state plans accurately reflect public opinion.[13]

The first thing established by the data is that, as of the 1990s, the American public was highly skeptical of the efficacy of the current welfare system (see figure 2).[14] When asked if the system of public welfare works well in this country or not, only a quarter of the

---

13. For details of the compilation, see Weaver, Shapiro, and Jacobs (1995).

14. The specific questions are as follows, each with a bit of an explanation before the question. ABC/*Washington Post* asked, "Overall would you say the system of public assistance works well in this country, or not?" They also asked, "Do you think the present system of public assistance discourages people from working, or do you think it helps them until they begin to stand on their own?" The National Opinion Research Center, General Social Services, asked, "First, . . . are we spending too much, too little, or about the right amount on . . . welfare?"

Figure 2   Changing Public Opinions about Welfare

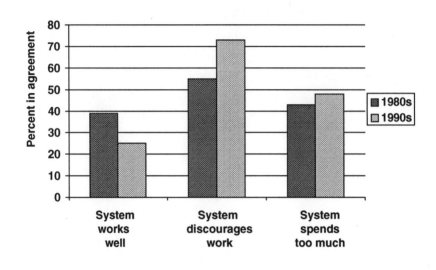

SOURCE: Weaver et al. 1995.

respondents felt it was working well in 1995, down from almost 40 percent a decade before. A large part of the problem, as isolated by these respondents, was that the system discouraged people from working, a sentiment that was growing until the 1996 reforms. That the reforms would occur, then, and would place an emphasis on work, should be of no surprise. Other aspects of the reforms are broadly popular as well. Eighty-nine percent of the population approved of the two-year limit, after which able recipients must get a job. And a similar majority seems to have developed in the mid-1990s for experimentation with welfare reform at the state level.

Disgust with the system as a whole did not necessarily translate into desires for benefit cuts, perhaps explaining why few states have ever seriously cut benefits. Survey results have generally found majorities lacking in response to whether we are spending too much on welfare, as highlighted in the figure. There has been a rise in the belief that welfare spending is too high, however, and in 1995 a majority indicated that we were indeed spending too much. This finding seems to be more linked to a disgust with the present system than with any decline in compassion among the public. Although the public supports cutting the present welfare system and the Food Stamps Program, the less-specific programs of "assistance to the poor," "helping poor children," "helping homeless people," and "providing food for low-income families" all continue to enjoy broad majority support. Furthermore, 60 percent of the population is willing to "pay more in taxes in order to provide job training and public service jobs for people on welfare so that they can get off welfare."

Public opinion is indeed one of the reasons why states would be reluctant to cut welfare benefit levels dramatically. There simply is no popular desire to do so. State politicians and the public as a whole are compassionate to children and to people who are down on their luck. Their compassion ends, however, when welfare becomes a way of life. That appears to have been the motivation behind the 1996 reforms, mandating that adults on welfare must find employment within two years and that their lifetime benefit be limited to five years. The public and politicians don't want to cut benefits as much as they want to end welfare as a way of life.

Political and Bureaucratic Institutional Limitations

The second reason states are unlikely to cut benefit levels is that there are significant bureaucratic and political institutional structures administering and supporting current policies and levels of welfare. Elected officials, interest groups, and bureaucrats all have an interest in meeting public opinion and in providing a workable transition from welfare to work.

Neither political party wants to be blamed for an ineffective or barbaric welfare system a few years down the road. It may presently be argued that Democrats are more compassionate in wanting to continue the safety net for the disadvantaged who are down on their luck; likewise, it may be argued that Republicans are the only ones willing to take the necessary steps to end welfare as we know it by encouraging or even forcing welfare recipients to finally enter the workplace. Indeed the reforms are going to be politically charged. We are in an era in which a majority of the state governments are divided, without single-party control of the governor and both houses of the legislature. The individual preferences of politicians within these parties lead to even more division. As such, proposals to cut welfare benefits significantly, as well as proposals for dramatic innovation, will face great difficulty.

Interest-group involvement may serve to complicate the political decisions further. Welfare-related interest groups such as the American Public Welfare Association and the Children's Defense Fund have played a significant role in federal aid decisions over the past few decades. They will now continue that role in the state capitals, joined by a variety of state-specific groups. Among their top priorities is ensuring that the benefit levels of individuals receiving aid will not be cut. Beyond that goal, these groups take an interest in promoting the well-being of the disadvantaged and will thus push for the types of innovations they view as most effective in helping these individuals find their way into employment with enough pay to allow them to support their families.

Yet another complexity in the political reform process comes from the bureaucratic institutional structure surrounding welfare in the various states. At the highest level of the welfare bureaucracies in many states are welfare boards that play an advisory or policy-forming role. Evidence (Volden 1995) suggests that these boards have in the past used information and proposal power to resist benefit cuts both in the face of declining federal aid and in response to increasing welfare rolls. The welfare bureaucracies closest to the people consist of a mass of caseworkers who are lifelong employees, often little swayed by legislated changes in policies or turnover of administrators. Evelyn Brodkin

(1996) studied the responses of these caseworkers throughout the Chicago area to a number of state-level policy changes. She found that welfare recipients do desire work-related services but that caseworkers are often restricted in their abilities to provide effective services. Workers are forced into playing "a numbers game," spending their time meeting state requirements rather than helping people. They are burdened by constant, rapid turnover of departmental executives and program managers, often finding it easier to ignore their new supervisors and to continue business as usual than to keep altering their practices time and again. And they are dealing with a clientele that is highly skeptical about state-administered services based on their dealings with the welfare system. As these two studies indicate, the bureaucracy surrounding welfare may resist benefit cuts but it also limits policy innovations.

The combination of public preferences and institutional inertia has kept states from seriously cutting benefit levels up to this point. With media attention focused on state welfare reform plans, it is unlikely that many states will decrease their benefit levels as a result of the 1996 welfare reforms. Interest groups, concerned citizens, workers in welfare programs and related volunteer services, and the media are all ready to lambaste any governor or legislature whose main aim seems to be cutting welfare benefits. Making such cuts at this time would be extremely costly politically. State budgetary savings are much more likely to come from the numbers of individuals taken off welfare down the road, after they have used up their benefit eligibility. At issue will be whether these transitions from welfare to work will be smooth or rocky. All indications are that the public, interest groups, and other politicians are willing and able to hold policymakers responsible for those programs that do not perform adequately, those that increase poverty, homelessness, and children's hunger.

Can the States Be Trusted?

The 1996 welfare reforms boost the incentives for state governments to decrease the number of people on welfare in their states. States will reap financial rewards either from cutting benefit levels or from help-ing (or forcing) recipients off welfare. In this chapter I have argued that governors and state legislators are constrained in their decisions by public opinion, interest groups, and the welfare bureaucracy. Although they have allowed welfare benefit levels to decline in value due to inflation, they have resisted making raw benefit cuts. This pattern will continue under the present welfare reforms. Although the benefit lev-els will still decline slightly in real value owing to our present low levels of inflation, we are unlikely to see state politicians propose or support broad across-the-board cuts in welfare.

The more significant effect of this legislation will come from the need to enroll a sizable portion of welfare recipients in work-related programs and from the reinforced desire of recipients to find employ-ment. The old welfare programs provided disincentives for work on multiple levels. The disadvantaged individuals on welfare often found that, if they took jobs, their benefit levels declined so rapidly that they weren't much better off. And states found that, if they promoted wel-fare-to-work programs that were successful, they would receive a de-cline in their grants from the federal government because fewer people were on the welfare rolls. We now have an opportunity to align these interests. States benefit from moving individuals from welfare to work, with fewer people on the welfare rolls and yet no decline in the size of the block grant. Recipients benefit from seeking and gaining employ-ment, especially in the face of deadlines and declining payments. In-terest groups and the public also favor this transition from welfare to work, with public opinion supporting increased spending for job train-ing even if it means higher taxes.

But this simple alignment of preferences does not automatically translate into a solution to the problems of unemployment and welfare in America. There will be pain. The initial proposals and experiments in many, if not most, of the states are likely to fail.[15] Two years down the road we are likely to see a rise in the number of homeless individuals and families that need to find shelter and additional assistance, often resorting to private organizations. Many of these situations will be the result of program glitches and bureaucratic errors. There will be a public outcry, and pressure will be placed on politicians to remedy what will be called a crisis. If the "crisis" does not arise within the next few years, it most certainly will come with the next recession, when states find that their increasing welfare rolls are not accompanied by sizable increases in federal grants. Governors and state legislatures will look to those states that have been most successful to find solutions to their own problems.

State policymakers will be held responsible for welfare failures and will be praised for their successes. When problems arise, the public and the media will know, better than before, who should be held accountable. Realizing this, state governors and legislators will keep an eye on policy successes in the other laboratories of democracy. They will use the information available within their own states as to where their programs have worked and where they have failed. And they will need to be quickly responsive. Even now, state governments are preparing for the eventualities of hard times. Many are building up surpluses during the present period of growth and recovery, surpluses that could be used during the next recession as an alternative to turning again to the federal government.

Entrusting the states with welfare reform does indeed mean that state governments *could* cut benefits dramatically and that they *could* carelessly throw families off welfare and onto the streets. But this will

---

15. Perhaps all the successes will be limited by their inability to address the underlying causes of joblessness (Wilson 1996) or by our general unwillingness to make the hard decisions necessary for true reform (Handler 1995).

not happen. State governance is not devoid of compassion. Elected officials at the state level face the same requirement of responsiveness to the public that national politicians face. But they are also endowed with the information and the incentives that make them more immediately responsive to the needs of their states and communities than the federal government could ever be. For welfare reform to be successful, governments need to be innovative, reacting to public pressures and learning from one another. It is a role that only the state governments can properly play. But it will not be an easy role. Success will come not only from welfare recipients fearing the loss of welfare if they do not find suitable jobs but also from politicians fearing the loss of their jobs if they do not find suitable welfare reforms.

Bibliography

Albritton, Robert B. 1989. "Impacts of Intergovernmental Financial Incentives on State Welfare Policymaking and Interstate Equity." *Publius: The Journal of Federalism* 19 (spring): 127–41.

Boeckelman, Keith. 1992. "The Influence of States on Federal Policy Adoptions." *Policy Studies Journal* 20, no. 3: 365–75.

Brodkin, Evelyn Z. 1996. "The State Side of the 'Welfare Contract': Discretion and Accountability in Policy Delivery." Paper prepared for the American Political Science Association Convention, San Francisco, California.

Brown, Robert D. 1995. "Party Cleavages and Welfare Effort in the American States." *American Political Science Review* 89, no. 1: 23–33.

Dye, Thomas R. 1990. *American Federalism: Competition among Governments*. Lexington, Mass.: D.C. Heath and Company.

Freeman, Patricia K. 1985. "Interstate Communication among State Legislators Regarding Energy Policy Innovation." *Publius: The Journal of Federalism* 15 (fall): 99–111.

Gray, Virginia. 1973. "Innovation in the States: A Diffusion Study." *American Political Science Review* 67: 1174–85.

Handler, Joel F. 1995. *The Poverty of Welfare Reform*. New Haven: Yale University Press.

Hanson, Russell L., and John T. Hartman. 1994. *Do Welfare Magnets Attract?* University of Wisconsin at Madison: Institute for Research on Poverty.

Katz, Jeffrey L. 1996a. "Welfare: After 60 Years, Most Control Is Passing to the States." *Congressional Quarterly Weekly Report*, August 3, pp. 2190–96.

———. 1996b. "Welfare Overhaul Law: Provisions." *Congressional Quarterly Weekly Report*, September 21, pp. 2696–705.

Kollman, Ken, John H. Miller, and Scott E. Page. 1995. "On the Possibility of States as Policy Laboratories." Paper prepared for the American Political Science Association Convention, Chicago, Illinois.

Lutz, James M. 1987. "Regional Leadership Patterns in the Diffusion of Public Policies." *American Politics Quarterly* 15: 387–98.

Osborne, David. 1988. *Laboratories of Democracy.* Boston, Mass.: Harvard Business School Press.

Peterson, Paul E. 1995. *The Price of Federalism.* Washington, D.C.: Brookings Institution.

Peterson, Paul E., and Mark C. Rom. 1990. *Welfare Magnets: A New Case for a National Standard.* Washington, D.C.: Brookings Institution.

Peterson, Paul E., Mark C. Rom, and Kenneth F. Scheve Jr. 1996. "The Race among the States: Welfare Benefits, 1976–1989." Paper prepared for the American Political Science Association Convention, San Francisco, California.

Plotnick, Robert D., and Richard F. Winters. 1985. "A Politico-Economic Theory of Income Redistribution." *American Political Science Review* 79: 458–73.

Savage, Robert L. 1985. "Diffusion Research Traditions and the Spread of Policy Innovations in a Federal System." *Publius: The Journal of Federalism* 15 (fall): 1–27.

Tiebout, Charles. 1956. "A Pure Theory of Local Expenditures." *Journal of Political Economy* 64: 416–24.

Tweedie, Jack. 1994. "Resources Rather Than Needs: A State-Centered Model of Welfare Policymaking." *American Journal of Political Science* 38, no. 3: 651–72.

Volden, Craig. 1995. "State Government Responses to Federal Grants-in-Aid: An Analysis of AFDC." Paper prepared for the American Political Science Association Convention, Chicago, Illinois.

Walker, Jack L. 1969. "The Diffusion of Innovation among the American States." *American Political Science Review* 63: 880–99.

Weaver, R. Kent, Robert Y. Shapiro, and Lawrence R. Jacobs. 1995. "The Polls—Trends: Welfare." *Public Opinion Quarterly* 59: 606–27.

Wilson, William Julius. 1996. *When Work Disappears*. New York: Alfred A. Knopf.

Richard L. Revesz

CHAPTER THREE

Federalism and Environmental Regulation
A *Normative Critique*

Vesting control over environmental regulation at the federal level is most commonly justified in both the legal academic literature and the legislative arena by two normative rationales. First, advocates of federal control argue that in its absence interstate competition would result in a "race to the bottom." Second, they maintain that federal regulation is necessary to prevent interstate externalities (Stewart 1977; Dwyer 1995).

This chapter shows that the race-to-the-bottom justification is analytically flawed, at least as a general argument for federal minimum standards. In contrast, although the presence of interstate externalities provides an analytically unimpeachable argument for federal intervention in cases in which the states cannot engage in Coasian bargaining,[1] the federal environmental statutes have done little to mitigate such externalities and may in fact have exacerbated the problem.[2]

I am grateful for the comments of Vicki Been and Richard Stewart.

1. The impediments to such bargaining are explored in Revesz (1996).

2. I have dealt more extensively with some of the issues in this chapter in Revesz (1992, 1996).

The race-to-the-bottom rationale for federal environmental regulation posits that states will try to induce geographically mobile firms to locate within their jurisdictions, in order to benefit from additional jobs and tax revenues, by offering them suboptimally lax environmental standards. The ensuing competition has the same structure as a prisoner's dilemma: a noncooperative game with a dominant strategy that is socially undesirable. Because they cannot coordinate their actions, states rationally choose a standard of environmental protection that is undesirably lax.

The problem of interstate externalities arises because a state that sends pollution to another state obtains the labor and fiscal benefits of the economic activity that generates the pollution but does not suffer the full costs of the activity. Under these conditions, economic theory maintains that an undesirably large amount of pollution will cross state lines.

Although they are sometimes conflated, the race to the bottom and the problem of interstate externalities are analytically distinct. Interstate externalities can be prevented by limiting the amount of pollution that can cross interstate borders, thereby "showing" upwind states the costs they impose on downwind states. As long as the externality is eliminated, advocates of federal regulation concerned about controlling interstate externalities should not care whether the upwind state chooses to have poor environmental quality—a central concern of race-to-the-bottom advocates. Conversely, if an upwind state chooses a high level of environmental quality within its borders but encourages the sources in the state to have tall stacks and locate near the interstate border, so that the effects are felt only in the downwind state, the situation poses an interstate externality problem, not a race-to-the-bottom problem.

These two rationales are also distinct from, but sometimes confused with, public choice arguments for vesting responsibility for environmental regulation at the federal level. Such public choice arguments claim that state political processes undervalue the benefits of environmental regulation or overvalue the corresponding costs, relative to the federal process, and that the outcome of the federal process is socially more desirable. Even if there were no interstate externalities, or if industry were wholly immobile so that there could be no race to the bottom, environmental standards would still be more protective at the federal level if, as the public choice argument posits, environmental groups are more effective at this level. Conversely, the interstate externality and race-to-the-bottom arguments for federal environmental regulation may apply even if states properly value the benefits of environmental protection. The analysis of public choice issues surrounding federal environmental regulation is outside the scope of this chapter.

Assessing the Race-to-the-Bottom Rationale

Race-to-the-bottom advocates must clear an initial hurdle. If one believes that competition among sellers of, say, widgets is socially desirable, why is competition among states, as sellers of a good—the right to locate within their jurisdictions—socially undesirable?

Indeed, states sell location rights because, even though they might not have the legal authority to prevent firms from locating within their borders, such firms must comply with the fiscal and regulatory regime of the state in which they wish to locate. The resulting costs to the firms can be analogized to the sale price of a traditional good. If federal regulation mandating a supracompetitive price for widgets is socially undesirable, why should it be socially desirable to have federal regulation mandating a supracompetitive price for location rights, in the form of more-stringent environmental standards than those that would result from interstate competition?

It is easy to identify possible distinctions between a state as seller of location rights and sellers of widgets. These differences, however, do not provide support for race-to-the-bottom claims.

First, if individuals are mobile across jurisdictions, the costs that polluters impose on a state's residents will depend on who ends up being a resident of the state; the resulting supply curve is thus far more complex than that of a widget seller. In the context of environmental regulation, however, race-to-the-bottom claims have focused exclusively on the mobility of capital, thereby assuming, at least implicitly, that individuals are immobile. Moreover, it is not clear that individual mobility renders competition among states different from competition among widget sellers. Indeed, even if individuals move in search of the jurisdiction that has the level of environmental protection that they favor (Tiebout 1956; Bewley 1981), and if there is capital mobility, the choice of environmental standards can nonetheless be efficient (Oates and Schwab 1987).

Second, although a seller of widgets is indifferent to the effect of the sale price on the welfare of the good's purchaser, a state ought to be concerned about the interests of the shareholders of the polluting firm who reside in the jurisdiction, both as individuals adversely affected by pollution and as owners of capital adversely affected by the costs of meeting regulatory requirements. But this difference does not support race-to-the-bottom arguments. Indeed, if some of the regulated firm's shareholders did not reside in the regulating jurisdiction and if capital were immobile, a state could extract monopoly profits by setting suboptimally *stringent* standards, benefiting its in-state breathers at the expense of out-of-state shareholders. (If capital is mobile, competition eliminates this problem.) Nothing in this account provides support for the opposite proposition: that interstate competition leads to suboptimally lax standards.

Third, states are not subject to the discipline of the market. If a producer of widgets consistently sells at a price that does not cover its average costs, it will eventually have to declare bankruptcy. A state, in contrast, can continue in existence even if it recklessly compromises the health of its residents. This difference merely establishes that a state might undervalue environmental benefits. But such undervaluation can take place even if capital is not mobile; it is a public choice problem rather than a race-to-the-bottom problem.

Fourth, states do not sell "location rights" at a single-component price; they require that firms comply with a variety of regulatory standards and that they pay taxes. The resulting market is thus more complex than one involving the sale of a traditional good. For example, a jurisdiction that imposes a lax worker safety standard but a stringent pollution standard will be desirable for a labor-intensive nonpolluting firm, whereas a jurisdiction with stringent safety and lax pollution standards will be desirable for a capital-intensive polluting firm. It is far from clear, however, why this additional complexity in the market would make interstate competition destructive. Instead, the example suggests a desirable sorting out of firms according to the preferences of individuals in the various jurisdictions.

In sum, although the analogy between interstate competition for industrial activity and markets for traditional goods is not perfect, it raises serious questions about race-to-the-bottom claims. At the very least, it should require race-to-the-bottom advocates to bear the burden of identifying relevant differences between the two markets and explaining why they turn otherwise desirable competition into a race to the bottom.[3]

Quite to the contrary, and contrary to the prevailing assumption in the legal literature and in the legislative debates, the leading economic model of the effects of interstate competition on the choice of environmental standards shows that interjurisdictional competition leads to the maximization of social welfare, rather than to a race to the bottom. Oates and Schwab (1988) posit jurisdictions that compete for mobile capital through the choice of taxes and environmental standards. A

---

3. It is paradoxical that, in the environmental area, the generally accepted premise is that jurisdictions extract too low a price from firms. In the land use context, influential support exists for the proposition that the price that jurisdictions extract is too high (Been 1991).

higher capital stock benefits residents in the form of higher wages but hurts them as a result of the forgone tax revenues and lower environmental quality needed to attract the capital.[4]

In their model, individuals live and work in the same jurisdiction and there are no interjurisdictional pollution spillovers. Each jurisdiction produces the same single good, which is sold in a national market. The production of the good requires capital and labor and produces waste emissions. The various jurisdictions set a total permissible amount of emissions as well as a tax on each unit of capital. Capital is perfectly mobile across jurisdictions and seeks to maximize its after-tax earnings, but labor is immobile.[5]

Each individual in the community is identical in both tastes and productive capacity and puts in a fixed period of work each week, and everyone is employed. Additional capital raises the productivity of workers and therefore their wages.

Each jurisdiction makes two policy decisions: it sets a tax rate on capital and an environmental standard. Oates and Schwab show that competitive jurisdictions will set a net tax rate on capital of zero (the rate that exactly covers the cost of public services provided to the capital, such as police and fire protection). For positive net tax rates, the revenues are less than the loss in wages that results from the move of capital to other jurisdictions. In contrast, net subsidies would cost the

---

4. Cumberland (1979) argues that interstate competition can lead to detrimental results as a result of factors such as the excessive discounting of future damages but provides no argument for why this determination would be performed better at the federal level.

5. In a companion unpublished manuscript, they argue that their conclusion that competition among states produces efficient outcomes holds even if individuals are mobile (Oates and Schwab 1987). If individuals are mobile, they will sort out, as in the Tiebout model, by their preference for environmental protection. Individuals who are willing to trade off a great deal in wages for better environmental quality will move to jurisdictions that impose stringent controls on industry; individuals who attach less importance to environmental quality will go to dirtier areas.

jurisdiction more than the increase in wages that additional capital would generate.

In turn, competitive jurisdictions will set an environmental standard that is defined by equating the willingness to pay for an additional unit of environmental quality with the corresponding change in wages. Pollution beyond this level generates an increment to wage income that is less than the value of the damage to residents from the increased pollution; in contrast, less pollution creates a loss in wage income greater than the corresponding decrease in pollution damages.

Oates and Schwab show that these choices of tax rates and environmental standards are socially optimal. With respect to tax rates, one condition for optimality is that the marginal product of capital—the increase in the output of the good produced by an additional unit of capital—must be the same across jurisdictions. Otherwise, it would be possible to increase aggregate output and, consequently, aggregate social welfare by moving capital from a jurisdiction where the marginal product of capital is low to one where it is high. Because capital is fully mobile, the market will establish a single rate of return on capital equal to the marginal product of capital minus the tax on capital. The choice by competitive jurisdictions of a net tax of zero equalizes the marginal product of capital across jurisdictions and is therefore consistent with optimality.

With respect to environmental standards, competitive jurisdictions equate the marginal private cost of improving environmental quality (measured in terms of forgone consumption) with the marginal private benefit. For net tax rates of zero, the marginal private cost is, as noted above, the decrease in wage income produced by the marginal unit of environmental protection. This decrease is also the marginal social cost since it represents society's forgone consumption. Thus, instead of producing a race to the bottom, competition leads to the optimal levels of environmental protection.

So far the inquiry has not revealed support for the claim of systematic environmental underregulation in a regime without federal intervention. It is possible, however, that, in particular instances, the game theoretic interactions among the states would lead to underregulation absent federal intervention. In such cases, federal minimum standards would be desirable. But it is equally plausible that in other instances the reverse would be true: the game theoretic interactions among the states would lead to overregulation absent federal intervention. In such cases, federal regulation would be desirable as well, but in such cases federal *maximum* standards would be called for. Accordingly, there is no compelling race-to-the-bottom justification for across-the-board federal minimum standards, which are the cornerstone of federal environmental law.

As an example of such game theoretic interactions, consider, in the Oates and Schwab model, a situation in which states decide to impose a positive net tax rate on capital, perhaps because they cannot finance the provision of public goods through a nondistortionary tax, such as a head tax. In such a situation, environmental standards will be suboptimally lax because the jurisdiction will continue to relax these standards beyond the optimal level in order to benefit from the additional net tax revenue that results from attracting additional capital.

A corollary, however, is that environmental standards will be suboptimally stringent if a jurisdiction, perhaps because of the visibility that attaches to attracting a major facility, chooses a tax rate on capital that is less than the cost of the public services that capital requires. Under this scenario, the optimal strategy for the jurisdiction is to strengthen the environmental standards beyond the optimal level so as to reduce the negative fiscal consequences.[6]

Another study relaxes the assumptions of constant returns to scale and perfect competition, which are a cornerstone of the Oates and Schwab model (Markusen, Morey, and Olewiler 1993, 1995). Instead,

---

6. There is no consensus in the academic literature on whether, on average, states and localities tax or subsidize capital (Mieszkowski and Zodrow 1989).

it considers the effects of state regulation on an industry that exhibits increasing returns to scale, a condition generally associated with imperfect competition. The conclusions of the model are that, depending on the levels of firm-specific costs, plant-specific costs, and transportation costs, interstate competition can produce either suboptimally lax or suboptimally stringent levels of regulation. Similarly, if the market for location rights is composed of a sufficiently small number of states (as sellers of location rights) and a large number of firms (as purchasers of such rights), the result will be suboptimally stringent regulation, but, in the case of a large number of states and a sufficiently small number of firms, the reverse will be true. In summary, just as there are game theoretic situations in which interstate competition produces environmental underregulation, there are other plausible scenarios under which the result is overregulation.

But even if, left to their own devices, states systematically enacted suboptimally lax environmental standards, federal environmental regulation would not necessarily improve the situation. Race-to-the-bottom arguments appear to assume, at least implicitly, that jurisdictions compete over only one variable—in this case, environmental quality. Consider, instead, the problem in a context in which states compete over two variables—for example, environmental protection and worker safety. Assume that, in the absence of federal regulation, State One chooses a low level of environmental protection and a high level of worker safety. State Two does the opposite: it chooses a high level of environmental protection and a low level of worker safety protection. Both states are in a competitive equilibrium, with industry not migrating from one to the other.

Suppose that federal regulation then imposes on both states a high level of environmental protection. The federal scheme does not add to the costs imposed on industry in State Two but it does in State One. Thus, the federal regulation will upset the competitive equilibrium, and unless State One responds, industry will migrate from State One to State Two. The logical response of State One is to adopt less-stringent worker safety standards. This response will mitigate the magnitude of the industrial migration that would otherwise have occurred.

Thus, if a race to the bottom exists, federal environmental standards can have adverse effects on other regulatory programs, in this case, worker safety. On this account, federal environmental regulation is desirable only if its benefits outweigh the costs that it imposes by shifting the pernicious effects of interstate competition to other programs.

More generally, the presence of such secondary effects implies that federal regulation would not be able to eliminate the negative effects of interstate competition, if such negative effects existed. Recall that the central tenet of race-to-the-bottom claims is that competition will lead to the reduction of social welfare; the assertion that states enact suboptimally lax environmental standards is simply a consequence of this more basic problem. In the face of federal environmental regulation, however, states will continue to compete for industry by adjusting the incentive structure of other state programs.

So, for example, if states cannot compete over environmental regulation, they will compete over worker safety standards. One might respond by saying that worker safety should also be (and is) the subject of federal regulation. But states would then compete over consumer protection laws or tort standards or whatever. Even if all regulatory functions were federalized, the competition would simply shift to the fiscal arena, where the competition would lead to the underprovision of public goods. Thus, the reduction in social welfare implicit in race-to-the-bottom arguments would not be eliminated.

The race-to-the-bottom rationale for federal environmental regulation is, therefore, radically underinclusive (unless one believes that, for public choice reasons, the race is politically more constrained in areas other than environmental regulation). It seeks to solve a problem that can be addressed only by wholly eliminating state autonomy. In essence, then, race-to-the-bottom arguments are frontal attacks on federalism. Unless one is prepared to federalize all regulatory and fiscal decisions, it is far from clear that federal intervention in the environmental arena would mitigate the adverse social welfare consequences of a race to the bottom, if such a race existed.

Assessing the Interstate Externality Rationale

The discussion in this section focuses on the Clean Air Act, which is the statute designed to deal with the pollution that gives rise to the most serious problems of interstate externalities. It shows that, despite these problems, the statute has been an ineffective response to the problem of interstate externalities and that, to some extent, it has had counterproductive effects.

AMBIENT AND EMISSION STANDARDS

The core of the Clean Air Act consists of a series of federally prescribed ambient standards and emission standards. Ambient standards prescribe the maximum permissible concentration of pollutants in the air but do not directly constrain the behavior of individual polluters. The National Ambient Air Quality Standards (NAAQS) are the statute's centerpiece; they establish minimum levels of air quality that, in principle, must be met nationwide. In addition, under the Prevention of Significant Deterioration (PSD) Program, areas with air quality that is better than the NAAQS must meet a more stringent ambient standard consisting of a baseline—the level of air quality on the date that the first major facility in the area applies for a permit—plus an increment above that baseline. In contrast, areas with air quality worse than the NAAQS are subjected under the nonattainment provisions to interim less-stringent ambient standards designed to accomplish "reasonable further progress" toward the attainment of the NAAQS.

Emission standards, in contrast, impose enforceable limitations on individual sources. The federally prescribed emission standards for stationary sources include New Source Performance Standards (NSPS), which apply to certain categories of stationary sources, as well as standards for major new sources in PSD areas, set by reference to the best available control technology (BACT); standards for major new sources in nonattainment areas, set by reference to the lowest achievable emission rate (LAER); and standards for existing sources in nonattainment areas set by reference to reasonably available control technology (RACT). Emission standards for automobiles are also federally prescribed. In contrast, the states are primarily responsible for the choice of emission standards for existing sources (except as constrained by the RACT requirements) through State Implementation Plans (SIPs) designed to ensure that the states are meeting the ambient air-quality levels prescribed by the NAAQS.

The federal emission standards are not a good means by which to combat the problem of interstate externalities. These standards constrain the pollution from each source but do not regulate the number of sources within any given state or the location of the sources.

Similarly, the various federal ambient air-quality standards are not well targeted to address the problem of interstate externalities because they are both overinclusive and underinclusive. From the perspective of constraining interstate externalities at a desirable level, ambient standards are overinclusive because they require a state to restrict pollution that has only in-state consequences. Concern about interstate externalities can be addressed by limiting the amount of pollution that can cross interstate borders. Because some air pollution has only local effects, such externalities can be controlled even if the upwind state chooses to have poor environmental quality within its borders.

Conversely, the federal ambient air-quality standards are underinclusive from the perspective of controlling interstate externalities because a state could meet the applicable ambient standards but nonetheless export a great deal of pollution to downwind states because the sources in the state have tall stacks and are located near the interstate border. In fact, a state might meet its ambient standards precisely *because* it exports a great deal of its pollution.

The federal ambient and emissions standards could perhaps be justified as a second-best means by which to reduce the problem of uncontrolled interstate externalities. One might believe that by reducing pollution across the board they reduce interstate externalities proportionately.

Such a view, however, is incorrect as a matter of both theory and empirical observation. The amount of aggregate emissions is not the only variable that affects the level of interstate externalities. In particular, two other factors play important roles. The first is the height of the stack from which the pollution is emitted: the higher the stack, the lesser the impact close to the source and the greater the impact far from the source. Thus, absent a federal constraint, states have an incentive to encourage their sources to use tall stacks as a way to externalize both the health and the environmental effects of the pollution, as well as the regulatory costs of complying with the federal ambient standards.

Second, the level of interstate externalities is affected by the location of the sources. In the eastern part of the United States, where the problem of interstate pollution is most serious, the prevailing winds blow from west to east. Thus, states have an incentive to induce their sources to locate close to their downwind borders so that the bulk of the effects of the pollution is externalized. They can induce this result, for example, through the use of tax incentives or subsidies or through permit and zoning decisions.

The best evidence that states do indeed encourage sources to use tall stacks can be found in the provisions of the SIPs adopted by at least fifteen states in response to the enactment of the Clean Air Act in 1970. These SIPs allowed sources to meet the NAAQS by using taller stacks rather than by reducing emissions (Senate Committee on Public Works 1974; Ayres 1975). In those SIPs, the permissible level of emissions was an increasing function of the height of the stack.[7] If the stack was sufficiently high, the effects would be felt only in the downwind states and would therefore have no impact on in-state ambient air-quality levels. Through these measures, the states created strong incentives for their firms to externalize the effects of their sources of pollution.

It is true that states had an incentive to externalize pollution even before the enactment of the Clean Air Act in 1970 because, by encouraging tall stacks, states could make other states bear the adverse health effects of pollution. The 1970 provisions, however, created an additional incentive. By encouraging the use of tall stacks, states could also externalize the regulatory impact of the standards, thereby availing themselves, for example, of the opportunity to attract additional sources without violating the NAAQS.

Taller stacks entail higher costs of construction and, possibly, operation. It is therefore conceivable that a state that did not view the externalization of health effects as sufficient by itself to outweigh imposing such costs on in-state firms would reach a different conclusion when tall stacks led to the externalization of both health and regulatory impacts.

More generally, before 1970, the states had not developed extensive regulatory programs for controlling air pollution. The net benefits of taller stacks, if any, might not have been worth the institutional investment necessary to create a regulatory program to transmit incentives for such stacks. The Clean Air Act, by requiring states to prepare SIPs, gave them no choice but to create an institutional structure designed to regulate the emissions of industrial sources. With that structure in place, it became comparatively easier to encourage tall stacks.

In addition, the health benefits of reducing the impact of emissions on in-state ambient air-quality levels are external to the firm emitting the pollution. Thus, a firm will take such effects into account only if

---

7. See, for example, Georgia Rules and Regulations for Air Quality Control (1972).

required to do so by a regulator. In contrast, the regulatory benefits of reducing the impact on in-state ambient air-quality levels can be captured directly by the firms, which, by using taller stacks, need to invest less to reduce their emissions.[8] Whereas before 1970 firms would have expended resources in tall stacks only if required to do so by a state regulatory agency, after 1970 they had an independent incentive for pursuing such a policy.

It is therefore not surprising that the use of tall stacks expanded considerably after 1970. For example, whereas in 1970 only two stacks in the United States were higher than 500 feet, by 1985, more than one hundred and eighty stacks were higher than 500 feet and twenty-three were higher than 1,000 feet (Reitze 1991; Vestigo 1985). Although the ability of states to externalize pollution in this manner is now less of a problem as a result of a system of regulation of stack height that followed the 1977 amendments to the Clean Air Act, tall stacks remain a means by which excessive pollution can be externalized.[9]

In contrast to the experience with tall-stack provisions, it is difficult to find direct evidence concerning whether states also provided incentives for sources to locate close to their downwind borders because such incentives are unlikely to be reflected in regulatory documents. There is, however, literature suggesting that such incentives are present in the case of the siting of waste sites (Mank 1995; Wiygul and Harrington 1993–94; Ingberman 1995; Zimmerman 1994). It would thus not be implausible to believe that states acted in the same manner with respect to air pollution facilities.[10]

---

8. The savings can be substantial. For example, a study in the early 1970s, when tall-stack credits were most prevalent, showed that the cost of complying with regulatory requirements was between $60/kW and $130/kW for a new lime scrubber, as compared with between $4/kW and $10/kW for a tall stack (Senate Committee on Public Works 1974).

9. For discussion, see Revesz (1996).

10. Such incentives for externalization are not confined to the United States. For

In summary, far from correcting the problem of interstate externalities, the act's ambient and emission standards may well have exacerbated it.

ACID RAIN PROVISIONS

The acid rain provisions of the 1990 amendments are often hailed
as a means of reducing interstate externalities because acid rain is
produced by pollution that travels long distances. These provisions,
however, apply only to the two pollutants that lead to the formation of
acid rain: sulfur dioxide and nitrogen oxides. Further, they apply to
only one type of facility: electric utilities. Moreover, these provisions
are not structured to allocate emissions between upwind and downwind states in a desirable manner.

With respect to nitrogen oxides, the provisions set emission standards for new and existing sources. As discussed above, emissions standards are not a well-targeted means for controlling interstate externalities.

With respect to sulfur dioxide, the acid rain provisions establish a
system of grandfathered permits, under which existing emitters are
assigned, for free, a number of permits equal to their historical emissions, subject to certain constraints. These permits are tradeable in a
single national market.

Although, as a result of these constraints on the grandfathering of
permits, the acid rain provisions are likely to reduce the amount of acid
rain, particularly after the year 2000, they make no attempt to allocate
emissions between upwind states and downwind states in an optimal
way because the permits trade in a single national market. The acid
rain problem manifests itself primarily in the Northeast but is caused

example, in the 1970s, France had an effluent fee system for water pollution in regions
in which part of the pollution would affect neighboring countries (Unweltprobleme
des Rheins 1976).

primarily by emissions from the Midwest. Because the market is national, midwestern sources can buy, without restriction, permits from the West and the Northeast. Trades from the Northeast to the Midwest are particularly undesirable because the acid rain resulting from northeastern emissions affects primarily the Atlantic Ocean, where the environmental consequences are minimal, whereas the acid rain resulting from midwestern emissions affects primarily the Northeast, where the environmental consequences are far more serious. In fact, downwind states are attempting to prevent their sources from selling permits to upwind sources, though such measures may well be struck down on constitutional grounds.

INTERSTATE SPILLOVER PROVISIONS

Sections 110(a)(2)(D) and 126(b) of the Clean Air Act, which date to the 1977 amendments, are the most comprehensive means for controlling interstate spillovers. These provisions prohibit a state from "contribut[ing] significantly to nonattainment in, or interfer[ing] with maintenance by," any other state with respect to the NAAQS or "interfer[ing] with measures required by" any other state under the PSD program.

Unlike the federal ambient and emissions standards, the interstate spillover provisions are designed to prevent excessive pollution from crossing interstate borders. Unlike the tall-stack and acid rain provisions, they are designed to deal with the problem comprehensively. Unfortunately, however, both in resolving various threshold issues and in interpreting substantive questions under the interstate spillover provisions, the administrative practice and case law have rendered these provisions virtually useless as a means of constraining interjurisdictional externalities.

The Environmental Protection Agency (EPA), through the resolution of various threshold issues, has blocked the prospects of downwind states complaining about excessive upwind pollution in important ways. First, it has maintained that it cannot predict such impacts more than 50 kilometers (about 30 miles) from the source of the pollution and has summarily rejected the predictions made by downwind states on the basis of longer range models.[11] Thus, sections 110(a)(2)(D) and 126(b) have been of no use to downwind states challenging pollution from sources not immediately contiguous to their borders.

The second threshold issue relates to the treatment of pollutants that are transformed as they travel through the atmosphere. For example, increased sulfur dioxide emissions upwind have an effect downwind not only on ambient air-quality levels of sulfur dioxide but also on ambient air-quality levels of particulates. The EPA has consistently taken the position, which has been upheld by the courts, that the impact of transformed pollution need not be taken into account in evaluating whether the upwind pollution is excessive.[12] Thus, acid rain, an important manifestation of the problem of interstate pollution, has been largely outside the reach of sections 110(a)(2)(D) and 126(b).

Third, the EPA has not set a national ambient air-quality standard for sulfates (Ackerman and Hassler 1991), even though a relative consensus developed within the scientific community in the 1980s concerning the adverse environmental effects of acid rain (Kulp 1990; Lee 1981). Nor has the EPA promulgated regulations to combat regional haze,[13] despite a statutory obligation under section 169A to do so by 1979. Had the EPA done so, it would have been required by sections 110(a)(2)(D) and 126(b) to take into account the impact of upwind

---

11. See, for example, *New York v. EPA*, 716 F.2d 440, 443-44 (7th Cir. 1983); *New York v. EPA*, 710 F.2d 1200, 1204 (6th Cir. 1983).

12. See, for example, *New York v. EPA*, 716 F.2d 440, 443 (7th Cir. 1983); *New York v. EPA*, 710 F.2d 1200, 1204 (6th Cir. 1983).

13. See, for example, *New York v. EPA*, 852 F.2d 574, 578-79 (D.C. Cir. 1988), *cert. denied*, 489 U.S. 1065 (1989); *Vermont v. Thomas*, 850 F.2d 99, 103 (2d Cir. 1988).

Table 1   Taxonomy of Interstate Spillovers

	Violation without Upwind Pollution	*Violation with Upwind Pollution*
Category 1	No	No
Category 2	Yes	Yes
Category 3	No	Yes

emissions of sulfur dioxide on the downwind ambient air-quality levels of sulfates as well as their impact on regional haze.[14]

The EPA's interpretation of the substantive standards of sections 110(a)(2)(D) and 126(b) has helped render these provisions ineffective in controlling interstate externalities. It is useful in this regard to construct a three-category taxonomy defined by whether the downwind state would meet the federal ambient standards if it did not have to face pollution transported from the upwind state and whether the downwind state actually meets the federal ambient standards despite the upwind pollution.

In the first category, the downwind state would meet the federal ambient standards without the upwind pollution and meets these standards despite the upwind pollution. In the second category, the downwind state would not meet the federal ambient standards even if there were no upwind pollution and, of course, does not meet the standards with the upwind pollution. In the third category, the downwind state would meet the federal ambient standards in the absence of upwind pollution but does not meet these standards with the upwind pollution; here, the upwind pollution is the but-for cause of the violation of the federal ambient standards. This taxonomy is summarized in table 1.

---

14. See, for example, *New York v. EPA*, 852 F.2d 574, 578-79 (D.C. Cir. 1988), *cert. denied*, 489 U.S. 1065 (1989); *Vermont v. Thomas*, 850 F.2d 99, 104 (2d Cir. 1988); New York v. EPA, 716 F.2d 440, 443 (7th Cir. 1983); *New York v. EPA*, 710 F.2d 1200, 1204 (6th Cir. 1983).

As to each of these categories, two questions are relevant. First, should the federal government play a role in controlling the upwind pollution? Second, assuming that such a role is appropriate, how should the federal government determine the permissible amount of upwind pollution that can enter the downwind state?

In Category 1, absent a violation of the federal ambient standards—either the NAAQS or the PSD increments—the EPA has chosen to place no limits on the upwind pollution. In this situation, the upwind pollution will be unconstrained even if it leads to a violation of a *state* ambient standard in the downwind state that is stricter than the federal standard. Further, the upwind pollution will be unconstrained even if the downwind state has limited the emissions of its sources in order to preserve a margin for growth that will permit it to attract new industry. Finally, the upwind pollution will be unconstrained even if the downwind state has been unable to set a baseline under the PSD program, thereby constraining further environmental degradation, because no major source has applied for a permit.[15]

In Category 2 cases, where the upwind pollution exacerbates a violation of a federal ambient standard in the downwind state, the EPA has never found upwind pollution to meet the "significant contribution" standard and has given little guidance on what factors distinguish a "significant" contribution from an "insignificant" one. In cases involving a single upwind source, the EPA concluded that contributions of 1.5 percent and of 3.0 percent were not excessive.[16] It reached these conclusions with no analysis, apparently basing its determination on the fact that those percentages do not seem particularly large. Nor did the EPA engage in any inquiry as to the cumulative impacts of upwind emissions. In light of the large number of sources that are likely to

15. See, for example, *Air Pollution Control District v. EPA*, 739 F.2d 1071, 1085-88 (6th Cir. 1984); *Connecticut v. EPA*, 656 F.2d 902, 910 (2d Cir. 1981).

16. See, for example, *Connecticut v. EPA*, 696 F.2d 147, 165 (2d Cir. 1982); *Air Pollution Control District v. EPA*, 739 F.2d 1071, 1092-93 (6th Cir. 1984).

affect ambient air-quality levels in the downwind state, this approach is unprotective of the interests of downwind states.

In Category 3, the EPA has indicated that the plain meaning of the statutory phrase "prevent attainment" requires the agency to deem excessive any upwind pollution that was the but-for cause of a violation of the federal ambient standards in the downwind state. In the only case in which the situation was presented, however, the agency rejected the downwind claim, stating that it doubted the accuracy of the modeling analysis performed by the downwind state.[17]

In summary, three principal rules emerge from the administrative interpretations of sections 110(a)(2)(D) and 126(b), which have been uniformly upheld by the courts: upwind pollution is never constrained if the downwind state meets the federal ambient standards; upwind pollution that exacerbates a violation of the federal ambient standards in the downwind states is constrained only if the upwind sources "significantly contributes" to the violation; and upwind pollution that is the but-for cause of the violation of federal ambient standards in the downwind state is always constrained.

The combination of these rules leads to illogical and, in practice, unprotective results. Consider first the Category 1 case of a downwind state that is not violating the NAAQS or the PSD increments. The amount by which the downwind state's ambient air-quality levels are better than the federal ambient standards represents that state's margin for growth. If the downwind state is not able to attract new sources because, for example, it is experiencing a temporary economic downturn, the rules allow an upwind state to consume the downwind state's margin for growth without constraint. Indeed, the rules even allow an upwind state to consume the downwind state's margin for growth by amending its SIP to permit its existing sources to increase their emissions up to the point at which the federal ambient standards become

---

17. See *New York v. EPA*, 852 F.2d 574, 580 (D.C. Cir. 1988), *cert. denied*, 489 U.S. 1065 (1989).

constraining in the downwind state.[18] Once the air-quality levels in the downwind state reach the level of the federal ambient standards (with the help of the upwind state), the downwind state will be unable to attract any sources without requiring emission reductions from its existing sources. At the extreme, a downwind state with no existing industrial base would be precluded from ever acquiring one.

In contrast, if the downwind state consumes its margin for growth first, either by attracting new sources or by amending its SIP to allow existing sources to pollute more, any increase in the pollution that the upwind state sends downwind would be deemed a violation of sections 110(a)(2)(D) and 126(b). An upwind state without an industrial base at the time that the downwind state reaches the federal ambient standards might be effectively precluded by this rule from attracting any polluting sources in the future if, as a result of the state's geography, any in-state emissions would be likely to migrate downwind.

Accordingly, the margin for growth in the downwind state would be allocated on a "first-come, first-served" basis. Such rules of capture are undesirable; they create incentives for both upwind and downwind states to use the downwind state's margin for growth at a faster rate than is economically desirable and do not allocate this margin for growth to whichever state values it most highly.

The discussion so far has focused on a downwind state that intends to use its margin for growth for economic expansion. Instead, states might set state ambient standards that are more stringent than the federal standards because they attach more value to environmental protection. The federal environmental laws emphasize, as explicitly reflected in section 116 of the Clean Air Act, that federal standards are floors and not ceilings and that, with exceptions not relevant to this discussion, states remain free to enact standards that are more stringent than the federal standards. Indeed, more-stringent standards are unde-

---

18. Of course, this strategy can be followed only if it does not lead to a violation of the federal ambient standards in the upwind state.

sirable only if they are an effort to externalize to other states the costs of pollution control.

Under the current administrative and judicial approach, however, more-stringent state ambient standards can be used only to limit the emissions of in-state sources and cannot be invoked, under any circumstances, to constrain upwind emissions. Such a regime creates a disincentive for downwind states to have more-stringent state ambient standards; downwind states bear all the costs of such standards (the costs of tougher emissions limitations for in-state sources), but the upwind states can appropriate the benefit by taking the additional opportunities created for the externalization of pollution.

The administrative and judicial approach to Category 2 situations, in which the upwind pollution aggravates a violation of the federal ambient standards, also is misguided. In Category 2 cases, the downwind state would be unable to constrain the upwind pollution unless the pollution was deemed a "significant contribution" to the violation. Under the nonattainment provisions of the Clean Air Act, however, the downwind state has an obligation to reduce its emissions until it meets the NAAQS. Thus, absent a "significant contribution" from upwind sources, the full burden of pollution reduction falls initially on the downwind sources, even if upwind reductions would be far less costly.

But once the downwind state made sufficient improvements to meet the NAAQS were it not for the upwind pollution, the situation would change. The upwind pollution would then be the but-for cause of the violation of the NAAQS in the downwind state—a Category 3 problem. The upwind pollution would be enjoined as "prevent[ing] the attainment" of the NAAQS, even if the cost to the upwind state of doing so were wholly disproportionate to the cost to the downwind state of somewhat more stringent pollution controls. As already indicated, in cases in which all emissions from the upwind state have at least some impact downwind, such a rule would prevent any polluting activity in the upwind state. The downwind state, by reducing its emissions to the point at which it could meet the NAAQS in the absence of the upwind pollution, but no further, could effectively destroy the upwind state's industrial base.

In summary, of the three rules articulated by the EPA and the courts to address the problem of interstate spillovers, two are overly lenient. In contrast, the third is overly harsh; perhaps as a result of its harshness, the EPA has failed to apply it to any specific case.

Perhaps the best illustration of the inefficacy of the Clean Air Act's interstate pollution provisions is provided by a dispute in which Kentucky complained about excessive emissions from an electric utility just across the border in Indiana. The Indiana utility was emitting 6.0 pounds of sulfur dioxide per million Btus of heat input—a level that reflected no pollution controls at all. In contrast, the electric utility in Kentucky had spent $138 million installing scrubbers in order to meet a standard of 1.2 pounds per million Btus. Moreover, the Indiana utility consumed almost half the permissible pollution levels in parts of Kentucky. Nonetheless, despite the compelling nature of the facts, the downwind state lost its challenge.[19]

Conclusion

This chapter shows that the race-to-the-bottom argument is an unsound basis for supporting federal minimum standards and that the problem of interstate externalities has not been successfully addressed by the federal environmental statutes. Thus, there is a serious mismatch between the structure of the environmental statutes and the two most prominent normative justifications for federal intervention in the environmental area.

The chapter concludes by briefly reviewing the various plausible

---

19. See *Air Pollution Control District v. EPA*, 739 F.2d 1071, 1092-93 (6th Cir. 1984).

normative justifications for federal regulation and suggesting what forms of federal intervention are needed to address the pathologies that otherwise would result. Of course, space precludes a full analysis of these matters.

INTERSTATE EXTERNALITIES

The preceding discussion has focused on pollution externalities, principally air pollution that crosses state lines. The goal is to design a well-functioning system for adjudicating the claims of downwind states that takes into account not only whether the emissions of upwind sources are excessive but also whether their stack height and location are an effort to externalize the adverse effects of pollution (Revesz 1996).

A different form of externality arises in the case of endangered species. To the extent that such species are located in a particular state, the costs of protection are largely concentrated in that state, but certain benefits accrue nationally or, for that matter, globally.

Interstate externalities also arise as a result of existence (nonuse) values placed on natural resources by out-of-state citizens. Such existence values provide a powerful justification for federal control over exceptional natural resources such as national parks.

All three of these interstate externality rationales justify only limited federal intervention that is designed to internalize the externality. In contrast, much of federal environmental law, such as the NAAQS under the Clean Air Act, regulates purely local effects.

ECONOMIES OF SCALE

Advocates of federal regulation often maintain, though without much empirical support, that centralization has strong economies of scale advantages. The economies of scale argument is most plausible at the earlier stages of the regulatory process, particularly with respect to the determination, through risk assessment, of the adverse effects of particular pollutants. Indeed, there is little reason for this determination to be replicated in each state.

The force of the rationale, however, is far less compelling at the standard-setting phase. At this phase, not only are the savings from eliminating duplication of efforts likely to be much lower but centralization will have serious social costs. Indeed, different regions have different preferences for regulation, derive different benefits from improving environmental quality, and face different costs of environmental protection. Although in principle federal regulation could be attentive to these differences, in practice it is far more likely to be uniform.[20]

UNIFORMITY

As already discussed, federal environmental standards are generally minimum standards. The states remain free to impose more-stringent standards if they wish to. A few standards, however, which apply to mobile sources, principally automobiles, and pesticides, are both floors and ceilings: they preempt both more-stringent and less-stringent state standards. Uniformity of this sort can be desirable for product standards where there are important economies of scale in production. In such circumstances, disparate regulation would break up the national market for the product and be costly in terms of forgone economies of scale.

The benefits of uniformity, however, are far from compelling in the case of process standards, which govern the environmental consequences of the manner in which goods are produced rather than the consequences of the products themselves. Indeed, unlike the case of dissimilar product standards, there can be a well-functioning common

---

20. As discussed above, the Clean Air Act does impose disuniform ambient standards, determined by whether an area is covered by the PSD or nonattainment programs, but the differences are not explainable by the factors discussed above (Oren 1988).

market regardless of the process standards governing the manufacture of the products traded in the market.

Particularly in the European context, harmonization of environmental process standards is advocated as a means to deny a comparative advantage to states with lax environmental standards. But the costs of complying with environmental regulation, or, for that matter, the costs of complying with all regulations, are only one component of the total costs of production. Other components include a state's investments in infrastructure, health care, and education, as well as its access to raw materials, wages, and labor productivity. These factors, which can have a significant effect on production costs, are unlikely to be the subject of governmental harmonization efforts. Thus, rather than eliminating cost differences, the harmonization of environmental standards has the effect of conferring a competitive advantage on states that perform well on nonharmonizable components of costs.

PROTECTION OF MINIMUM LEVELS OF PUBLIC HEALTH

There is a powerful notion, informed in part by constitutional considerations, that a federal polity should ensure all its citizens a minimum level of environmental protection. This argument is frequently invoked by supporters of federal regulation (Stewart 1977). At some level, this justification is obviously compelling; a minimum level of health ought to count as a basic human right, in the same manner as minimum levels of education, housing, or access to employment. From the perspective of this justification, there are two problems with federal environmental regulation. First, regulation seeks to limit the risk of exposure to particular pollutants or from particular sources, rather than limiting aggregate levels of environmental risk. As a result, the approach is both overinclusive (it regulates more than the minimum that has a claim to quasi-constitutional legitimacy) and underinclusive (it makes no effort to determine aggregate exposure levels and therefore whether some individuals are in fact below the minimum).

Second, because environmental risks are only one component of health risks, it is difficult to understand, particularly in the United States, why the federal government has such a preeminent role with respect to environmental regulation when it does relatively little with respect to the provision of general health care. In fact, investments in health benefits such as immunizations or prenatal care would have a far larger impact on health than investments in environmental regulation. As a result, the justification for federal regulation based on the need to guarantee a minimum level of health calls for a radically different form of regulation than that currently in effect, one that focuses on total environmental health risks and the interactions among environmental health risks and other health risks. I realize, however, that such a strategy would require a fundamental rethinking of the current media-by-media approach to environmental regulation.

INTERNATIONAL TREATY OBLIGATIONS

Increasingly, domestic environmental regulation, for example in the case of ozone-depleting chemicals, is undertaken in response to international treaty obligations. To the extent that the federal government plays an exclusive role in international relations, it is probably desirable that the federal government should also bear primary responsibility for domestic regulation that implements treaty obligations.

ROLE OF PUBLIC CHOICE CONSIDERATIONS

Some commentators make normative claims against the devolution of federal responsibilities to the states on the grounds, based largely on the theory of collective action, that environmental interests will be relatively underrepresented at the state level (Swire 1996). If the theory of collective action is taken seriously, however, the existence of federal regulation would also be difficult to explain; concentrated industrial interests with large stakes in the outcome ought to overpower citizen breathers even at the federal level.

An extensive public choice literature suggests that the impetus for environmental regulation sometimes comes, implicitly or explicitly, from the regulated firms themselves, which, through rents and barriers to entry, obtain an advantage relative to other firms in the industry (Keohane, Revesz, and Stavins 1997). At other times, the advocates are particular regions of the country, which hope to obtain a comparative advantage with respect to other regions (Pashigian 1985). Thus, the lineup in the debates is as likely to be polluter versus polluter or regional interest versus regional interest as it is polluter versus breather.

When the relevant interactions are seen in this manner, the case for federal regulation on public choice grounds is considerably weakened. A more definitive conclusion on this question, however, must await further sustained analysis.

In summary, in a well-designed system, the allocation of authority between the federal government and the states would look very different than it does now. The federal government currently performs many functions that would better be discharged at the state level and fails to perform some functions that can only be effectively carried out at the federal level. Perhaps this gap results in part from confusion over the strength of the race-to-the-bottom and interstate externality justifications for federal environmental regulation, which this chapter hopes to help dispel.

References

Ackerman, Bruce A., and William T. Hassler. 1991. *Clean Coal/Dirty Air.* New Haven: Yale University Press.

Ayres, Richard E. 1975. "Enforcement of Air Pollution Controls on Stationary Sources under the Clean Air Amendments of 1970." *Ecology Law Quarterly* 4:441.

Been, Vicki. 1991. "Exit as a Constraint on Land Use Exactions: Rethinking the Unconstitutional Conditions Doctrine." *Columbia Law Review* 91:473.

Bewley, Truman F. 1981. "A Critique Theory of Local Public Expenditures." *Econometrica* 49:713.

Cumberland, John H. 1979. "Interregional Pollution Spillovers and Consistency of Environmental Policy." In *Regional Environmental Policy: The Economic Issues*, ed. Horst Siebert. New York: New York University Press.

Dwyer, John P. 1995. "The Practice of Federalism under the Clean Air Act." *Maryland Law Review* 54:1183.

Ingberman, Daniel E. 1995. "Siting Noxious Facilities: Are Markets Efficient?" *Journal of Environmental Economics and Management* 29:S-20.

Keohane, Nathaniel O., Richard L. Revesz, and Robert N. Stavins. 1997. "The Positive Political Economy of Instrument Choice in Environmental Policy." *Environmental Economics and Public Policy*, ed. Paul Portney and Robert Schwab. London: Edward Elgar, Ltd.

Kulp, J. Laurence. 1990. "Acid Rain: Causes, Effects, and Control." *Regulation*, winter 1990, p. 41.

Lee, Valerie. 1981. "Interstate Sulfate Pollution: Proposed Amendments to the Clean Air Act." *Harvard Environmental Law Review* 5:71.

Mank, Bradford C. 1995. "Environmental Justice and Discriminatory Siting: Risk-Based Representation and Equitable Compensation." *Ohio State Law Journal* 56:329.

Markusen, James R., Edward R. Morey, and Nancy D. Olewiler. 1993. "Environmental Policy When Market Structure and Plant Locations Are Endogenous." *Journal of Environmental Economics and Management* 24:69.

———. 1995. "Competition in Regional Environmental Policies When Plant Locations Are Endogenous." *Journal of Public Economics* 56:55.

Mieszkowski, Peter, and George R. Zodrow. 1989. "Taxation and the Tiebout Model: The Differential Effects of Head Taxes, Taxes on Land Rents, and Property Taxes." *Journal of Economic Literature* 27:1098.

Oates, Wallace E., and Robert M. Schwab. 1987. "Pricing Instruments for Environmental Protection: The Problems of Cross-Media Pollution, Interjurisdictional Competition and Interregional Effects." Manuscript, University of Maryland.

———. 1988. "Economic Competition among Jurisdictions: Efficiency Enhancing or Distortion Inducing?" *Journal of Public Economics* 35:333.

Oren, Craig N. 1988. "Prevention of Significant Deterioration: Control-Compelling versus Site-Shifting." *Iowa Law Review* 74:1.

Pashigian, B. Peter. 1985. "Environmental Regulation: Whose Self-Interests Are Being Protected." *Economic Inquiry* 23:551.

Rat von Sachverständigen für Umweltfragen. 1976. *Unweltprobleme des Rheins.* Stuttgart und Mainz: Verlag W. Kohlhammer GMBH.

Reitze, Arnold W., Jr. 1991. "A Century of Air Pollution Control Law: What's Worked; What's Failed; What Might Work." *Environmental Law* 21:1549.

Revesz, Richard L. 1992. "Rehabilitating Interstate Competition: Rethinking the 'Race-to-the-Bottom' Rationale for Federal Environmental Regulation." *New York University Law Review* 67:1210.

——. 1996. "Federalism and Interstate Environmental Externalities." *University of Pennsylvania Law Review* 144:2341.

Senate Committee on Public Works. 1974. "Clean Air Act Oversight: Hearings Before the Subcommittee on Environmental Pollution." 93d Cong., 2d Sess.

Stewart, Richard B. 1977. "Pyramids of Sacrifice? Problems of Federalism in Mandating State Implementation of National Environmental Policy." *Yale Law Journal* 86:1196.

Swire, Peter P. 1996. "The Race to Laxity and the Race to Undesirability: Explaining Failures in Competition Among Jurisdictions in Environmental Law." Symposium Issue. *Yale Law & Policy Review/Yale Journal on Regulation.* March.

Tiebout, Charles M. 1956. "A Pure Theory of Local Expenditures." *Journal of Political Economy* 64:416.

Vestigo, James R. 1985. "Acid Rain and Tall Stack Regulation under the Clean Air Act." *Environmental Law* 15:711.

Wiygul, Robert B., and Sharon C. Harrington. 1993–94. "Environmental Justice in Rural Communities Part One: RCRA, Communities, and Environmental Justice." *West Virginia Law Review* 96:405.

Zimmerman, Rae. 1994. "Issues of Classification in Environmental Equity: How We Manage Is How We Measure." *Fordham Urban Law Journal* 21:633.

Roberta Romano

CHAPTER FOUR

State Competition for Corporate Charters

Introduction

Federalism is a central feature of U.S. corporate law. Corporate law, which involves the relation between a firm's shareholders and managers, is a subject matter preserved for the states. Corporations choose their legal regime from the fifty states and the District of Columbia by their choice of state of incorporation. There is no physical connection to the choice: a firm's statutory domicile is established by a paper filing in the office of the chosen domicile's Secretary of State. The states' legislative approach is primarily enabling; corporate codes supply standard contract terms for corporate governance. Code provisions are default terms for corporate charters that can be customized to meet particular needs (such as changing a default majority voting rule to a supermajority rule for a firm with a block holder who wants veto control).

Corporate code contents are quite varied, from specifying minor matters, such as the number of days between the notice and holding of a meeting, to more important ones, such as the procedures for corporate combinations. States typically provide a different set of default rules, called close corporation codes, for small, privately held firms. Different defaults are necessary because small firms' governance problems differ from those of large public corporations, where the key concern is the separation of ownership and control, which creates the possibility that the nonstock-holding managers may run the firm to promote their own interests rather than those of the shareholders. The variety in corporation codes and their enabling approach accommodates the diversity in organization, capital structure, and lines of business among for-profit firms.

U.S. corporate law presumes that firms should be run in the shareholders' interests; profit maximization or, in a world of uncertain cash flows, maximization of equity share prices is the goal. There are persuasive explanations for this. First, in competitive markets, maximizing share value allocates resources efficiently and thereby maximizes social welfare (e.g., Varian 1992). Second, even if different shareholders have different preferences for saving over consumption, owners' utility is maximized when the firm maximizes share prices because those wanting to consume can trade against the increased value of the shares without affecting firm policy and hence are not in conflict with those who wish to save (e.g., Brealey and Myers 1991, 21). This renders shareholder interests more homogeneous than the interests of other participants in firms, such as employees, reducing the cost of collective decisions (Hansmann 1988). Finally, because equity investments are residual claims (lowest in priority in insolvency), with no maturity date or fixed income guarantee, they are more vulnerable than the investments of other firm participants (who periodically must renegotiate their claims and can protect their claims by express contracting) and need the more open-ended protection of corporate law (Williamson 1984).

The conjunction of a shareholder wealth-maximizing objective and the separation of ownership and control in large public corporations means that corporate codes, to be effective, must mitigate the agency problem created by the separation of ownership and control. As this chapter indicates, federalism has worked to ensure that, for the most part, provisions in corporate codes are in the shareholders' interests.

It must be noted, however, that there are important areas involving shareholder-manager relations that are subject to national government control. The federal securities laws regulate the issuance and trading of securities and the continuing disclosure responsibilities of public firms.[1] In addition, a variety of federal laws prevent financial institutions from holding large blocks of equity investments and actively monitoring management (Roe 1994). In contrast to state corporate codes, the federal laws are mandatory. As will be noted, the legislation with arguably the most adverse impact on corporate governance is in fact federal, not state, legislation.

Delaware and the Competition for Charters

Firms typically incorporate locally or in Delaware; approximately half of the largest corporations are incorporated in Delaware, and the overwhelming majority of firms changing their state of incorporation move to Delaware (Dodd and Leftwich 1980; Romano 1985). As a consequence, a substantial portion of Delaware's tax revenue is derived from incorporation fees (also referred to as business franchise taxes), which are assessed according to outstanding shares of incorporated firms. From 1960 to 1995, franchise fees averaged more than 16 percent of Delaware's total tax revenues (see table 1). Delaware's dominance in incorporations is extremely stable; it has been the leading incorporation state since the 1920s.

New Jersey, however, was, the initial leader in the charter market.

---

1. Securities Exchange Act of 1934, 15 U.S.C. § 78a et seq.; Securities Act of 1933, 15 U.S.C. § 77a et seq. These laws do not preempt the states from additionally regulating securities transactions. In practice, however, the states have exempted large public corporations (those listed on a national stock exchange) from their securities laws.

Table 1   Delaware's Revenues from Corporate Charters, 1960–1995

Year	Franchise Taxes ($000)	% of Total Tax Collected
1960	9,864	13.7%
1961	12,621	16.3
1962	13,579	14.9
1963	13,977	14.3
1964	15,635	15.5
1965	15,790	13.1
1966	14,091	10.9
1967	17,615	12.6
1968	21,414	14.8
1969	20,572	13.1
1970	43,924	22.5
1971	55,212	24.9
1972	49,129	19.1
1973	50,777	17.7
1974	57,073	18.5
1975	55,030	16.4
1976	67,887	18.9
1977	57,949	14.8
1978	60,509	13.5
1979	63,046	12.8
1980	66,738	12.9
1981	70,942	12.9
1982	76,591	12.9
1983	80,031	12.5
1984	92,270	12.9
1985	121,057	14.8
1986	132,816	15.0
1987	152,152	15.4
1988	180,583	17.7
1989	195,862	17.3
1990	200,201	17.7
1991	203,868	17.5
1992	297,004	22.1
1993	284,839	21.3
1994	307,008	21.3
1995	336,348	21.2
AVERAGE		16.2%

SOURCE: U.S. Bureau of the Census, *State Government Tax Collections* (Washington, D.C.: Government Printing Office, 1960–1995).

Delaware's succession was largely due to historical accident in that it was well situated to take over the incorporation business after New Jersey radically revised its corporation code under the influence of the Progressive Party and lame-duck Governor Woodrow Wilson, who was about to become president. At the time of the reform, changes in New Jersey's economy had reduced the importance of incorporation revenues in its budget (Grandy 1989). Delaware had previously adopted New Jersey's code and recognized its case law as binding precedent.[2] A few years later, New Jersey tried to regain its preeminent position in the charter market, as state politics once again changed, by repealing the Progressives' corporate law reforms, but was unable to do so; the firms that had switched to Delaware when New Jersey's Progressives revised the corporate code stayed put.[3]

There is evidence that states compete with Delaware for the chartering business. For example, corporate law innovations diffuse across states in an S-shaped curve (the proportion of adopters increases with time), similar to technological innovations, which is interpreted as a sign of powerful competition (Romano 1985, 233–35; Carney 1996). In addition, state franchise revenues are significantly positively related to the responsiveness of a state's corporate legal system to firm demands (measured as a function of the rate and extent to which legal innovations considered desirable by reincorporating firms are enacted) (Romano 1985: 236–41). Finally, firms migrate from states with low levels of responsiveness to those with higher levels (Romano 1985, 246–47).

Because reincorporating firms—firms that change their state of incorporation—are the drivers of state competition (as the marginal

---

2. *Wilmington City Ry. Co. v. People's Ry. Co.*, 38 Del. Ch. 1, 47 A. 245 (Del. Ch. 1900).

3. New Jersey's changed financial situation that made it less reliant on franchise revenues, which, as explained below, is a crucial reason for Delaware's sustained market dominance, would have deterred reincorporations because it rendered it difficult for firms to be confident that New Jersey would not change its code to their disadvantage again.

purchasers their demand shapes the suppliers' responses in the charter market), it is important to understand their motivation. Firms reincorporate because they anticipate undertaking transactions such as an acquisition, that will be cheaper under the new state's law than that of the original incorporation state (Romano 1985). A legal regime can reduce such transaction costs directly (for example, Delaware does not require a vote by acquiring firm shareholders in stock acquisitions) and indirectly, by affecting the prospect of litigation. When a firm expects a change in activity that increases the likelihood of shareholder litigation, which is true of the principal transactions motivating a reincorporation (Romano 1985), specific characteristics of a legal regime become important, such as the presence of a well-developed body of case law and explicit indemnification rules, for they facilitate doing business by permitting transactions to be structured with greater certainty concerning potential liability. Delaware's legal regime is preeminent in delivering these features; in no other state can a firm obtain a legal opinion on a proposed transaction with such ready availability and predictability. This is not fortuitous; it is part and parcel of the process by which Delaware is predominant in the corporate charter market.

Delaware's extraordinary success in the corporate charter market has been the source of a recurring corporate law debate on the efficacy of federalism. In one of the most cited articles in the *Yale Law Journal* (Shapiro 1991), William Cary (1974) contended that Delaware's heavy reliance on incorporation fees led it to engage in a "race for the bottom" to adopt laws that favored managers' over shareholders' interests. Cary did not discuss the reincorporation process and the fact that a shareholder vote is required to accomplish a domicile change; as he criticized Delaware's code for delegating decisions to managers away from shareholders, he must have believed that shareholders are ignorant of their interests with respect to the choice of legal regime but not other business transactions. The evidence he provided in support of his thesis was the staffing of the Delaware judiciary with prominent members of the corporate bar, and an analysis of judicial opinions in which he concluded that federal court decisions were fairer to shareholders than were those of the Delaware state courts. Cary advocated the enactment of federal corporate law standards that would preempt state codes by establishing a floor for shareholder protection.

Ralph Winter (1977) identified a crucial flaw in Cary's analysis: firms are embedded in a series of markets—capital, labor, product, and corporate control—that constrain managers' domicile choices. Winter maintained that firms operating under a legal regime that did not maximize shareholder wealth would be outperformed by firms operating under one that did and that the former firms' correspondingly lower stock prices would subject their managers to job displacement through takeover or insolvency. Thus, even if managers choose the incorporation state, their choice will follow shareholders' interest. Given the power of the logic of Winter's critique, more-recent critics of state competition stress that market imperfections prevent the alignment of managers' interests with those of the shareholders and that externalities make states the improper jurisdictional unit, that is, corporation codes affect third parties outside the manager-shareholder relation who are also nonresidents of the domiciliary state and thus not part of its legislative calculus (e.g., Bebchuk 1992). Before turning to the empirical evidence to arbitrate the debate, the source of Delaware's long-standing success must be specified more precisely.

Why Is Delaware the Leading Incorporation State?

Delaware's preeminence in the charter market is a function of its ability to resolve credibly the commitment problem of relational contracting. A corporate charter is a relational contract; it binds the state and firm in a multiperiod relationship in which their respective performance under the contract is not simultaneous. A corporate code must be continually revised and updated as business conditions change and new issues arise that could not be foreseen and specified in the initial code provisions. After a firm is incorporated in a state and pays the franchise fee, the state may fail to update its code or may alter its code in ways unfavorable to the firm; the firm is stuck up to the point where the cost of moving falls below the cost of operating under an inferior code. In other words, the firm is in a vulnerable contracting position made worse by the fact that the party with whom it is contracting—the state—is also the enforcer of the contract. Because the firm may have no bona fide legal recourse for breach, it will look for, and the state will need to provide some credible means of, a committment to uphold the contract and maintain it (that is, update it) in ways that do not exploit the firm. The state's interest in doing this is franchise revenues. For if a state cannot commit to a code that reduces the cost of doing business, firms will be reluctant to pay a fee for that right or to do business with a particular state, as opposed to another provider, in the first place.

Delaware's commitment mechanism depends on its substantial investment in assets that have no alternative use at any comparable value than in maintaining its corporate chartering business. These assets are (1) a reputation for responsiveness to corporate concerns, (2) a comprehensive body of corporate case law, (3) administrative expertise in the expeditious processing of corporate filings, and (4) judicial expertise in administering corporate law. Unlike other states, corporate law cases in Delaware are tried in only one court, the chancery court, facilitating the development of judicial expertise. In addition, corporate law specialists are routinely appointed to the Delaware Supreme Court.

Delaware's intangible reputational asset is related to the substantial revenue Delaware receives from the franchise tax: because such a large proportion of its budget is financed from incorporations and it is a small state with very limited indigenous revenue sources, there is no ready substitute to which Delaware can turn to maintain the level of services it provides its citizens in the absence of a vigorous incorporation business. This makes Delaware as vulnerable to the firms as they are to it; it has too much to lose from failing to maintain a responsive corporation code. Because it is a hostage to its own success, Delaware is able to make credible its commitment to corporate law responsiveness.

Delaware's legal capital is not only a commitment device but also a primary attraction for reincorporating firms. It provides predictability for business planning for firms that will be undertaking complicated transactions such as acquisitions. The development of legal capital also feeds back into the development of its reputational capital, enhancing Delaware's credible precommitment to firms, just as the number of incorporated firms feeds back into the development of legal capital. The more firms that incorporate in Delaware, the more comprehensive the case law becomes as more issues are litigated. The more comprehensive the case law, the more firms will incorporate locally. The more firms incorporated, the higher the state's reliance on franchise fees to finance its operations. And the greater the reliance on fees, the more credible the commitment to responsiveness. The large number of firms already located in Delaware not only feeds back into the development of Delaware's legal and reputational capital but also cements its position; it gives Delaware a first-mover advantage in the charter market.

In addition to its hostagelike assets of limited redeployability, Delaware's constitution requires changes to the corporation code to be approved by a supermajority of both state legislative houses (Article IX, § 1). This provision is another commitment device for it makes it difficult for Delaware to reverse the direction of its code. It increases the likelihood that the legal regime can be no worse than it was at the time of incorporation, which is desirable if corporations are risk averse with respect to the legal system and adopt a strategy toward the choice of incorporation state that minimizes the worst case. It does not appear to slow corporate law reform as Delaware is one of the leading innovators, as well as imitators of corporate law reforms (Romano 1985); this is probably due to the legislature's reliance on the corporate bar

(Moore 1987, 780). The constitutional provision also serves to preserve the value of the personal investments made by Delaware citizens in developing skills to service Delaware corporations. History underscores the importance of this provision as not all of the New Jersey senate votes enacting the Progressives' corporate law reforms that cost it its chartering business met Delaware's supermajority requirement (Romano 1993a, 42). Only a critical election revolutionizing state politics could produce a radical reversal in Delaware's corporate law policy that would lead to firms' massive migration out of state.

It would be extremely difficult for any state to unseat Delaware in the chartering business, since Delaware has a first-mover advantage in offering a credible commitment in terms of reputation and case law from its starting point of a large number of incorporated firms. However, Delaware remains vigilant. It continually updates its code (both by innovating and by copying others) and seeks new business. Despite Delaware's overwhelming lead, other states do, in fact, appear to compete to retain the incorporations that they have, as well as to lure business away (Blackman 1993; Carney 1996; Harlan 1988; Romano 1985, 233–42). And this is key to the successful operation of the system. None of the essential attributes would be present in a national chartering regime; given the size of the federal budget, franchise fees will not provide the federal government with enough financial incentive to be responsive to firms rather than behaving opportunistically. In addition, there would be no competition prodding the federal government to improve its service, unless the costs of incorporating in a foreign country, or of operating as an unincorporated entity, are considerably reduced from present levels.

Critics who propose replacing the federal system of corporate charters with national chartering either in whole or in part (Cary 1974; Schwartz 1976; Bebchuk 1992) ignore the key incentive features of state competition. Their proposals presuppose not only that competition is malevolent but also that Congress would enact more shareholder-friendly laws than the states. There is, however, scant support for the proposition that national politics would be for the better. The organizational advantages of managers over shareholders are just as strong at the national level as at the local level, so if the problem is a political market failure, shifting the arena will not solve it (Romano 1988). It is also questionable whether any of the existing national laws affecting corporate governance benefit shareholders (see, e.g., Roe 1994 [financial institution stock ownership regulation]; Haddock and Macey 1987 [insider trading regulation]; Easterbrook and Fischel 1983 [proxy regulation]; Benston 1973 [disclosure regulation]; Schwartz 1986 [tender offer regulation]). In fact, the most severe restriction on investors' choice of governance structure—the prevention of large block holding by U.S. financial institutions—has occurred largely in the national political arena (Roe 1994), not in the states.

The takeover setting is potentially different from other issues involving shareholder-manager relations because bidders, who are directly affected by corporation codes, are not typically represented in the legislating state. In addition, some commentators contend that takeovers adversely affect employees and creditors. Bidders are, however, represented in Delaware; it is the domicile of more acquirers than any other state (Romano 1987, 141, 143), and its takeover statutes have been more favorable to bidders than those of other states (Romano 1993a, 59). Moreover, the bulk of the evidence on takeovers does not support the other externality claims concerning employees and creditors (Romano 1992, 136–42). Finally, the federal takeover legislation has not been terribly friendly to bidders. Although we can craft a theoretical argument for national regulation of takeovers based on potential externalities, in practice, as noted, the national political process will not mitigate the problem (for details, see Romano [1988] and Romano [1993a, 75–84]). It is instead likely to exacerbate the problem as there will be no safety valve for shareholders to invest in firms in a competing jurisdiction that has rules more favorable to bidders as in the current federal system (as is true of the laws of California and Delaware).

Who Benefits from State Competition?

The explanation of Delaware's dominance in the states' competition
for corporate charters does not resolve the debate over who benefits,
managers or shareholders, from this competition. This is because its
explanation of the incentives for states to respond to firms' demand for
particular corporate law innovations does not depend on who in the
firm sets that demand. However, it meshes better with a system in
which shareholders benefit from competition. Given the extraordinary
variety in investment opportunities with which issuers of equity must
compete for funds, it is questionable whether the specialized assets
contributing to Delaware's success would have much value, or whether
a first-mover advantage could be sustained, if the output of the process
was a legal regime adverse to shareholder interests.

Macey and Miller (1987) contend that a third group has benefited
from state competition: the Delaware corporate bar, which is best situated among the political interest groups in Delaware to obtain legislation that enhances its share of Delaware's chartering business profits
(through, for instance, enacting legislation facilitating shareholder litigation). It is a highly organized interest group with a cost advantage
over other groups—it has to master corporate law for its livelihood. As
Macey and Miller note, to the extent that the bar's influence simply
involves redistribution among Delaware citizens of the fees that firms
pay for a Delaware charter, the bar's interest in corporate codes is not
of much concern from the standpoint of advocates of federalism in the
state competition debate. More important, state competition will limit
the extent to which the Delaware bar can support a legal regime that
shifts value away from investors. Corporations pay close attention to
legal costs; in-house counsel exert considerable time and effort on controlling legal expenses. They are also in a position to become knowl-
edgeable about differences in litigation regimes and can propose rein-

corporation in a state with rules less hospitable to litigation if Delaware favors the bar excessively to firms' detriment.

An empirical literature, originating in the 1980s, attempts to answer the question, are investors better or worse off from their firms' changing incorporation state or, more generally, from their having the option to do so under the federal system of charter competition? The question of whether the Delaware bar benefits at corporations' expense has not been examined empirically. The most typical methodological approach to arbitrate the state competition debate uses standard financial econometrics to investigate the impact of new information — referred to as an event — on stock prices. Studies using such a technique are called event studies and are comprehensively reviewed in Brown and Warner (1985). The information effect (that is, investors' opinion) of an event will be picked up in the residuals of a stock price regression, which uses a pricing model that adjusts for marketwide movements. A significantly positive (negative) residual, which is also referred to as an abnormal return, indicates that the event under study is beneficial (harmful) to shareholders' interests.

Event Studies of the Impact of State Competition

The best evidence on whether state competition benefits shareholders consists of event studies of reincorporations (Hyman 1979; Dodd and Leftwich 1980; Romano 1985; Bradley and Schipani 1989; Netter and Poulsen 1989; Wang 1996). Examining the price effects of a change in statutory domicile is equivalent to studying who benefits from state competition. This is because reincorporating firms are the marginal corporate charter consumers whose actions drive the market, and a price reaction will measure the market's response to the firms' new legal regime. Measured over a variety of time periods and samples of firms, the reincorporation event studies find either a significant positive price effect or no significant price effect on firms' reincorporations. No study observes negative stock price effects.

Netter and Poulsen (1989) subdivide their sample of firms reincorporating in Delaware into firms emigrating from California, which they consider a "shareholder rights" state because takeover defensive tactics permitted in Delaware are prohibited in California, and firms emigrating from other states. The firms migrating from California experience insignificant positive returns and there is no significant difference in abnormal returns across the two samples. Wang (1996) divides his sample into firms reincorporating in Delaware and those reincorporating in other states. He finds that only the Delaware subsample experiences significant positive abnormal returns. Taken together, the six studies suggest that the market considers reincorporation to be a beneficial event for shareholders.

There is, however, an interpretative question concerning these results that involves confounding events. Is the positive stock price revaluation due to the change in domicile or to anticipated changes in the corporation's business following reincorporation? To investigate this possibility, Romano (1985) subdivided her sample of reincorporating firms according to anticipated transactions on reincorporation; the subsets of firms moving to engage in acquisitions and of those moving for tax and miscellaneous reasons experienced significant positive returns, whereas the abnormal returns of the subset moving to engage in takeover defenses were insignificant. These results are consistent with event studies of the reincorporation-precipitating transactions alone; announcements of acquisition programs produce positive abnormal returns (Schipper and Thompson 1983), whereas defensive tactics have mixed results of significantly negative, positive, or insignificant abnormal returns (Jarrell, Brickley, and Netter 1988). Analysis of variance of the abnormal returns across the three groups of reincorporating firms, however, indicated that the group differences are not statistically significant.

Although the event studies of reincorporations provide the best measure of whether state competition benefits investors, event studies of statutory enactments and judicial decisions may also be probative, subject to some important interpretive caveats. Because much of corporate law is enabling, a particular statute or judicial decision may not produce a significant stock price effect if the studied firms (as opposed to the specific litigant) can cheaply transact around the rule or will otherwise not be affected by it (for example, the rule involves takeover defenses and the sample firms have a low probability of becoming a target). In addition, investors may accurately anticipate case outcomes and legislative enactments. This undermines the methodology by rendering incorrect the date the researcher has identified as an event because the expectations' prior impounding in the price ensures that no stock price reaction will be observed on the event date. This is a particularly serious concern for event studies of judicial decisions because the Delaware legislature has expeditiously overturned controversial decisions (Romano 1992). To the extent that investors expect such legislative reversals, there will be no stock price reaction to court decisions. This renders it difficult to test whether a judicial decision is significantly adverse to investor interests. Not surprisingly, in contrast to the uniformity of findings in the reincorporation event studies, the event studies of these other phenomena have disparate results.

The most widely studied state law phenomenon is the enactment of takeover statutes, which are intended to make hostile takeovers difficult. Because shareholders receive substantial premiums in takeovers, legislation that reduces the likelihood of a successful takeover should adversely affect firms' stock prices. The findings of studies of the stock price effects of takeover statutes, however, vary: many find significantly negative effects (Broner 1987; Ryngaert and Netter 1988; Karpoff and Malatesta 1989 and 1995; Schumann 1989; Sidak and Woodward 1990; Mahla 1991; Szewczyk and Tsetsekos 1992), while others find the effect is insignificant (Margotta and Badrinath 1987; Romano 1987 and 1993b; Margotta, McWilliams, and McWilliams 1990; Pugh and Jahera 1990; Jahera and Pugh 1991). The two most comprehensive studies, aggregating between forty and forty-nine statutes enacted in more than twenty states, find significantly negative, albeit small, abnormal returns (Karpoff and Malatesta 1989; Mahla 1991). Much, but not all, of these differences can be explained by the type of takeover statute under study. The statutes less likely to constrain hostile bids (fair price and other constituency statutes) tend to produce insignificant abnormal returns, whereas the more severely restrictive statutes (disgorgement, control share acquisition, and business combination freeze statutes) have significant negative price effects.

The aggregate takeover statute data are the strongest evidence against state competition; they suggest that federalism in corporate law adversely affects investors. But even here the strength of such a conclusion is rendered problematic when all the evidence is carefully reviewed. A key finding in the studies of takeover statutes from the standpoint of state competition is that the adoption of Delaware's statute, which is less restrictive of takeover bids than other states' laws, had no significant stock price effect (Karpoff and Malatesta 1989; Jahera and Pugh 1991).[4] Delaware was also a laggard, not a leader, in adopting takeover regulation. One reason for this distinction is that many state takeover laws are enacted at the behest of a domestic firm that is the target of a hostile bid (Butler 1988; Romano 1987 and 1988, 461), and in Delaware, no one firm has enough influence over the legislature to be able to obtain instant statutory protection. The state competition dynamic is therefore clearly different for takeover statutes than for other

---

4. The insignificance is not likely due to anticipation of legislation after the Supreme Court upheld the constitutionality of state takeover statutes in *CTS Corp. v. Dynamics Corp. of America*, 481 U.S. 69 (1987) against charges of their burdening interstate commerce or being preempted by federal securities law. Jahera and Pugh (1991) provide a time line of the events surrounding the statute's enactment that undermines an anticipation explanation. The first public announcement of the bar's consideration of a statute occurred one month after the *CTS* decision; two weeks later it was announced that the bar had decided not to propose legislation. The first public announcement of a revival of legislation, which took a different form from the statute under consideration after *CTS*, occurred more than five months later.

corporate law reforms, and Delaware has not been at the forefront of legislation.

The event studies of judicial corporate law decisions are closely related to the takeover statute research. Two studies investigated the effect of Delaware and other state court decisions concerning a specific takeover defensive tactic—poison pills[5]—on the litigants or firms that were takeover targets (Kamma, Weintrop, and Wier 1988; Ryngaert 1988). These studies find significant negative price effects on decisions upholding the defensive tactic and significant positive price effects on decisions invalidating it. As with the enactment of takeover statutes, the negative effect of decisions upholding takeover defenses evinces that state competition is an imperfect safeguard of equity interests. The third study, by Weiss and White (1987), examined the stock price effect on all Delaware-incorporated firms of seven Delaware Supreme Court decisions, four of which involved mergers and one of which involved a hostile takeover defense. They found no significant price reaction to any of the decisions. This result can be considered evidence of the importance of the market anticipation and transactional planning caveats to event study data interpretation because, read in conjunction with the other two studies, we find that judicial decisions affect share values of the *litigants* (for whom the transaction's structure has already been fixed), not firms in general. Weiss and White, however, interpret their data as evidence that investors are not concerned about state law differences and that consequently states do not compete for charters.

---

5. A poison pill is a shareholder rights plan triggered on a hostile bid that enables target shareholders to acquire senior securities in the target or common shares in the bidder at a substantial discount.

Performance Comparisons across Incorporation State

Three studies examine whether the choice of legal regime affects corporate performance. Because statutory domicile is an endogenous choice, if firms choose their incorporation state to maximize share values (that is, firms match legal regimes with anticipated transactions), we should not expect to find cross-sectional performance differences. And, indeed, none of the studies finds differences in performance.

Baysinger and Butler (1985) compare return on equity across firms incorporated in states with "strict" codes (codes that limit management discretion, identified by the outflow of firms to Delaware) and firms headquartered but not incorporated in those states. They find no difference in performance across the two groups. Romano (1996) reports further results on this issue, to compensate for two limitations in Baysinger and Butler's study, the data-driven definition of strict code states and a simple performance measure. She examines changes in earnings (before extraordinary income and taxes), standardized by assets, for reincorporating firms before and after reincorporation, compared to all other firms in their industry and to a paired sample of nonreincorporating firms not domiciled in Delaware. The reincorporating firms' relative performance is positive compared with the industry average, but there is no statistically significant difference in performance for the reincorporating firms as a whole or grouped by the transaction motivating the move. Wang (1996) also finds no statistically significant difference in postreincorporation earnings performance for reincorporating firms and a matched sample of nonreincorporating firms. Among the reincorporating firms, firms reincorporating in Delaware outperformed their industry while the firms reincorporating in other states did not, but none of the differences are significant.

Finally, a large number of firms that reincorporate in Delaware cannot be included in reincorporation event studies because they rein-corporate shortly before their initial public offering (IPO). Using post-reincorporation performance data is, in fact, the only means to exam-ine the impact of the choice of domicile for these firms. Romano (1996) finds that IPO domicile has no measurable effect on perfor-mance (measured by stock return over varying intervals after the IPO).

There is no evidence in the performance data to suggest that state competition is adverse to shareholders' interests. The performance data are consistent with the view that the charter market is in equilibrium; firms select the legal regime that enables them to reduce their transac-tion costs and thereby attain their best possible performance.

The Uniqueness of the U.S. Corporate Law Regime

The federal chartering system, with its clear benefits to shareholders, is a unique feature of U.S. corporate law. Other federations—the Euro-pean Union (EU) and Canada—have limited or no competition for charters (Daniels 1991; Romano 1993a: 118–40; MacIntosh and Cumming 1996). Competition is absent in the EU primarily because of the choice-of-law rule for corporations' internal affairs; unlike the statutory domicile rule of the United States and other common law legal systems, European countries follow the law of a corporation's real or effective seat, which requires a significant physical presence in the state for the domicile choice to be effective. Because of the substantial cost of reincorporation under a real seat rule, the pool of recruitable corporations is sparse; EU members thus have reduced incentives to compete for charters by offering responsive codes. There is, further, little incentive for the EU to change the choice-of-law rule because the corporation laws of important members, such as Germany, have objec-tives other than shareholder wealth maximization. Such a regime would be undermined in a competitive system because the interests of equity investors will dominate the choice of incorporation state in that their capital is the most mobile of the firms' participants.

Charter competition is attenuated across Canadian provinces principally because provincial governments are unable to control their corporation laws. Security administrators, whose jurisdiction is based on shareholder residence and not issuer domicile, can regulate corporate governance and can override provincial corporate law regimes. In addition, the Supreme Court of Canada reviews all provincial appellate court decisions. The overlapping of jurisdiction weakens a province's incentive to invest in the necessary nonredeployable assets that ensure Delaware's success because the value of such assets can be impaired without recourse by security administrators or the Supreme Court. It also limits the ability of a province to commit to a responsive code. Moreover, firms have less of a reason to invest in optimizing incorporation decisions, as the fate of even a code of a province acting in the utmost good faith is uncertain. This further diminishes provincial incentives to compete.

An additional difference that may affect the likelihood of charter competition is the preponderant corporate ownership structure. In contrast to U.S. public corporations whose stock is typically diffusely held, most European and Canadian corporations have controlling block holders. Such firms may be less interested in many of the features of a legal regime on which states compete; a code offering organizational flexibility and managerial discretion, for example, is not of value to a shareholder manager who has voting control and can run the firm as he wishes. Concomitant with this difference, shareholder lawsuits are more difficult to bring in Canada and Europe than in the United States and shareholder rights are more limited.

Another way to understand the difference is to note that in the absence of charter competition, equity must be concentrated to compensate for a legal regime less responsive to shareholder interests by more intensive monitoring of management. The absence of charter competition in the EU and Canada thus does not necessarily indicate that shareholders in those countries should earn lower rates of return than U.S. investors. Corporate organization adapts to the legal environment. If, in a world of global product market competition the cost of capital is cheaper when corporate ownership is diffuse, however, facilitating charter competition may well become a policy initiative for those nations.

Conclusion

U.S. corporate law is unique among federal political systems. State competition has produced innovative corporate codes that quickly respond to changing market conditions and firm demands. Corporate law commentators have debated whether this responsiveness benefits shareholders. The best available evidence indicates that, for the most part, the race is for the top and not the bottom in the production of corporate laws. Still, the direction is not linear. The enactment of takeover statutes, which negatively affect shareholder wealth, demonstrates that state competition is not perfect. Perfection is not, however, the appropriate standard for measuring the legislative output of state competition. In the short run, there will inevitably be deviations from the optimum in a federal system. But in the longer run, competitive pressures are exerted when states make mistakes. For example, after Pennsylvania enacted a restrictive takeover statute, the majority of firms opted out of its provisions in response to shareholder dissatisfaction with them, and other states did not enact similar statutes (Romano 1993a, 68–70). Such self-correcting pressure is absent from a centralized national system. It is instructive, in this regard, that a study of the noncompetitive context of the EU harmonization project for corporate laws found that European nations have a panoply of restrictive provisions long eliminated from U.S. codes as unwieldy and unprofitable (Carney 1996). There is no reason to believe that, where state laws are inadequate, a national corporate law would be better, and there is some reason to believe that it would be worse.

The answer to the question of whether state competition is efficacious then lies between the Cary (race for the bottom) and Winter (race to the top) positions but far closer to the Winter end of the spectrum. There is, to repeat, no evidence that changing statutory domicile and hence state competition harms shareholders, and there is substantial evidence that a domicile change is a wealth-increasing event, although the positive price effects may be a function of the market's evaluation of anticipated transactions rather than the value of the new domicile itself. Corporate law is a policy domain in which federalism has worked well. It has fostered the productive use of the corporate form to do business and may well have facilitated the development of thick capital markets and firms in which ownership and control are separated.

References

Baysinger, Barry D., and Henry N. Butler. 1985. "The Role of Corporate Law in the Theory of the Firm." *Journal of Law and Economics* 28: 179–91.

Bebchuk, Lucian A. 1992. "Federalism and the Corporation: the Desirable Limits on State Competition in Corporate Law." *Harvard Law Review* 105: 1437–1509.

Benston, George. 1973. "Required Disclosure and the Stock Market: an Evaluation of the Securities Exchange Act of 1934." *American Economic Review* 63: 132–55.

Blackman, Peter. 1993. "Move over Delaware!" *New York Law Journal,* December 16, pp. 5–6.

Bradley, Michael and Cindy Schipani. 1989. "The Relevance of the Duty of Care Standard in Corporate Governance Law." *Iowa Law Review* 75: 1–74.

Brealey, Richard, and Stewart Myers. 1991. *Principles of Corporate Finance.* 4th ed. New York: McGraw Hill.

Broner, Adam. 1987. "New Jersey Shareholders Protection Act: an Economic

Evaluation, a Report to the New Jersey Legislature." Office of Economic Policy, State of New Jersey.

Brown, Stephen J., and Jerold B. Warner. 1985. "Using Daily Stock Returns: the Case of Event Studies." *Journal of Financial Economics* 14: 401–38.

Butler, Henry N. 1988. "Corporation-Specific Antitakeover Statutes and the Market for Corporate Charters." *Wisconsin Law Review* 1988: 365–83.

Carney, William J. 1996. Federalism and Corporate Law: A Non-Delaware View of the Results of Competition. In *International Regulatory Competition and Coordination*, eds. Joseph McCahery, William W. Bratton, Sol Picciotto, and Colin Scott. Oxford: Clarendon Press.

Cary, William L. 1974. "Federalism and Corporate Law: Reflections upon Delaware." *Yale Law Journal* 83: 663–707.

Daniels, Ronald J. 1991. "Should Provinces Compete? The Case for a Competitive Corporate Law Market." *McGill Law Journal* 36: 130–90.

Dodd, Peter, and Richard Leftwich. 1980. "The Market for Corporate Charters: 'Unhealthy Competition' versus Federal Regulation." *Journal of Business* 53: 259–83.

Easterbrook, Frank H., and Daniel R. Fischel. 1983. "Voting and Corporate Law." *Journal of Law and Economics* 26: 395–427.

Grandy, Christopher. 1989. "New Jersey Corporate Chartermongering, 1875–1929." *Journal of Economic History* 49: 677–92.

Haddock, David, and Jonathan R. Macey. 1987. "Regulation on Demand: A Private Interest Model with an Application to Insider Trading Regulation." *Journal of Law and Economics* 30: 311–52.

Hansmann, Henry. 1988. "Ownership of the Firm." *Journal of Law, Economics, and Organization* 4:267–304.

Harlan, Christi. 1988. "Massachusetts Bill Seeks Courts for Business." *Wall Street Journal*, December 9, p.B6.

Hyman, Allen. 1979. "The Delaware Controversy—the Legal Debate." *Delaware Journal of Corporate Law* 4: 368–98.

Jahera, John S., and Pugh, William N. 1991. "State Takeover Legislation: The Case of Delaware." *Journal of Law, Economics, and Organization* 7: 410–27.

Jarrell, Gregg A., James A. Brickley, and Jeffry M. Netter. 1988. "The Market for Corporate Control: The Empirical Evidence since 1980." *Journal of Economic Perspectives* 2: 49–68.

Kamma, Sreenivas, Joseph Weintrop, and Peggy Wier. 1988. "Investors' Perceptions of the Delaware Supreme Court Decision in *Unocal v. Mesa.*" *Journal of Financial Economics* 20: 419–30.

Karpoff, Jonathan, and Paul Malatesta. 1989. "The Wealth Effects of Second Generation State Takeover Legislation." *Journal of Financial Economics* 25: 291–322.

———. 1995. "State Takeover Legislation and Share Values: the Wealth Effects of Pennsylvania's Act 36." *Journal of Corporate Finance* 1: 367–82.

Macey, Jonathan R., and Geoffrey P. Miller. 1987. "Toward an Interest-Group Theory of Delaware Corporate Law." *Texas Law Review* 65: 469–523.

MacIntosh Jeffrey G., and Douglas Cumming. 1996. "The Role of Interjurisdictional Competition in Shaping Canadian Corporate Law." Manuscript, University of Toronto Faculty of Law.

Mahla, Jr., Charles R. 1991. "State Takeover Statutes and Shareholder Wealth." Ph.D. dissertation, University of North Carolina.

Margotta, Donald G., and Swaminathan Badrinath. 1987. "Effects of the New Jersey Shareholder Protection Legislation on Stock Prices." Manuscript, Northeastern University.

Margotta, Donald G., Thomas P. McWilliams, and Victoria B. McWilliams. 1990. "An Analysis of the Stock Price Effect of the 1986 Ohio Takeover Legislation." *Journal of Law, Economics, and Organization* 6: 235–51.

Moore, Andrew. 1987. "State Competition: Panel Response." *Cardozo Law Review* 8: 779–82.

Netter, Jeffry, and Annette Poulsen. 1989. "State Corporation Laws and Shareholders: The Recent Experience." *Financial Management* 18, no. 3: 29–40.

Pugh, William N., and John S. Jahera. 1990. "State Antitakeover Legislation and Shareholder Wealth." *Journal of Financial Research* 13: 221–31.

Roe, Mark J. 1994. *Strong Managers Weak Owners: The Political Roots of American Corporate Finance.* Princeton: Princeton University Press.

Romano, Roberta. 1985. "Law as a Product: Some Pieces of the Incorporation Puzzle." *Journal of Law, Economics, and Organization* 1: 225–83.

———. 1987. "The Political Economy of Takeover Statutes." *Virginia Law Review* 73: 111–99.

———. 1988. "The Future of Hostile Takeovers: Legislation and Public Opinion." *University of Cincinnati Law Review* 57: 457–505.

———. 1992. "A Guide to Takeovers: Theory, Evidence and Regulation." *Yale Journal on Regulation* 9: 119–79.

———. 1993a. *The Genius of American Corporate Law.* Washington, D.C.: AEI Press.

———. 1993b. "Comment: What Is the Value of Other Constituency Statutes to Shareholders?" *University of Toronto Law Journal* 43: 533–42.

———. 1996. "Corporate Law and Corporate Governance." *Industrial and Corporate Change* 5: 277–339.

Ryngaert, Michael. 1988. "The Effect of Poison Pill Securities on Shareholder Wealth." *Journal of Financial Economics* 20: 377–417.

Ryngaert, Michael, and Jeffry Netter. 1988. "Shareholder Wealth Effects of the Ohio Antitakeover Law." *Journal of Law, Economics, and Organization* 4: 373–83.

Schipper, Katherine, and Rex Thompson. 1983. "Evidence on the Capitalized Value of Merger Activity for Acquiring Firms." *Journal of Financial Economics* 11: 85–119.

Schumann, Laurence. 1989. "State Regulation of Takeovers and Shareholder Wealth: the Case of New York's 1985 Takeover Statutes." *RAND Journal of Economics* 19: 557–67.

Schwartz, Alan. 1986. "Search Theory and the Tender Offer Auction." *Journal of Law, Economics, and Organization* 2: 229–53.

Schwartz, Donald E. 1976. "A Case for Federal Chartering of Corporations." *Business Lawyer* 31: 1125–59.

Shapiro, Fred R. 1991. "The Most-Cited Articles from the Yale *Law Journal.*" *Yale Law Journal* 100: 1449–64.

Sidak, J. Gregory, and Susan Woodward. 1990. "Corporate Takeovers, the Commerce Clause, and the Efficient Anonymity of Shareholders." *Northwestern University Law Review* 84: 1092–1118.

Szewczyk, Samuel H., and George P. Tsetsekos. 1992. "State Intervention in the Market for Corporate Control: the Case of Pennsylvania Senate Bill 1310." *Journal of Financial Economics* 31: 3–23.

Varian, Hal R. 1992. *Microeconomic Analysis.* 3d ed. New York: W.W. Norton.

Wang, Jianghong. 1996. "Performance of Reincorporated Firms." Manuscript, Yale School of Management.

Weiss, Elliott, and Lawrence White. 1987. "Of Econometrics and Indeterminacy: A Study of Investors' Reactions to 'Changes' in Corporate Law." *California Law Review* 75: 551–607.

Williamson, Oliver E. 1984. "Corporate Governance." *Yale Law Journal* 93:1197–1230.

Winter, Ralph K. 1977. "State Law, Shareholder Protection, and the Theory of the Corporation." *Journal of Legal Studies* 6: 251–92.

PART THREE

John A. Ferejohn and
Barry R. Weingast

CONCLUSION

The Politics of the
New Federalism

The renewed interest in federalism raises concerns about policy as well as constitutional law, as policymakers and researchers have begun to ask whether the devolution of some programs to the states might result in better policy. These inquiries are, necessarily, guided by the analysis of specific issues of the kind exhibited in this volume. But such inquiries are also political, involving elected officials, parties, ideologies, and interest groups operating at all levels of American government. In brief, they involve the voters deciding the detailed character of the federal system.

This is as it should be. Federal authority expanded over the states and localities as a result of Democratic Congresses creating a wide variety of new programs over the past half century. With the sanction of a pliable Supreme Court, Congress either preempted state authority or enlisted state agencies in the service of federal programs. This expansion of federal authority over the states—most recently in the form of unfunded mandates—helped generate a political reaction against federal intrusion and a willingness to expand the powers of the states.

Indeed, many profound changes in the allocation of federal authority have already begun to flow from recent electoral outcomes at both the federal and the state level. These changes, which have taken place at all levels of government, involve judges as well as political officials. Moreover, they do not all point in the direction of the devolution of federal authority. Two cases revealing a more complex pattern of new federalist thinking are the continued expansion of federal criminal law, much of it with bipartisan support, and the recent Republican-led effort to regulate state tort law and limit punitive damage awards.

In recent years, judges and legal academics have begun to ask whether the constitutional jurisprudence that formed the basis of New Deal and Great Society legislation is constitutionally defensible. This inquiry is both broad, involving many policies simultaneously rather than one at a time, and deep, addressing the fundamental powers of the national government and, indirectly, that of the states.

Two events have greatly enlivened the debate about the appropriate powers and reach of the national government. The first involves the "new federalism" initiatives unveiled in the 104th Congress that attempted to turn a variety of regulatory and police powers back to the states. The second concerns the Supreme Court's decision in *Lopez* (1995), suggesting that it may reconsider limits on the national government under the commerce clause.

Although many of the new federalist initiatives originated in the 104th Republican Congress, some Democrats also believe that federalism can enhance public performance. Alice Rivlin, for example, argues that federalism provides a means of "reviving the American dream."[1] But although *Lopez* and the 1996 welfare reform legislation have attracted the most public attention, they are not isolated occurrences. Both Congress and the Supreme Court have evidenced an increasing willingness to rethink the relationship between federal and

---

1. Alice Rivlin, *Reviving the American Dream: The Economy, the States, and the Federal Government* (Washington, D.C.: Brookings Institution, 1992).

state authority and to revisit fundamental assumptions about the nature of American government.

For example, in a number of areas, Congress has begun to experiment with a kind of "statutory federalism" in which the states are permitted wider discretion within federal statutory schemes. The welfare reform legislation adopted in 1996 illustrates this effort. That legislation grants the states' vastly increased authority to craft their own welfare policies; further, Congress provides a substantial grant of funds for this purpose. This bloc grant is, in principle, supposed to permit each state to define its own welfare program free of federal interference. Nonetheless, Congress retains the power to regulate state plans. And Congress did restrict state plans in that legislation, attempting to ensure that states enforce welfare time limits and make progress toward moving welfare recipients into the workforce. Obviously, the success of statutory federalism depends greatly on Congress's willingness to abstain from micromanaging state policy processes. Yet it is by no means clear that either Democratic or Republican members of Congress will, or can, restrain themselves.

Since the *Garcia* decision, the Supreme Court has begun exploring ways to define a new constitutional federalism that curtails the domain of congressional authority. This effort has two prongs. The first, seen in *Lopez*, is aimed at limiting Congress's commerce clause powers. Although too soon to tell, this thrust may in time extend beyond the commerce clause to encompass the spending clause. The second prong of constitutional federalism is aimed at giving meaning to the Tenth Amendment. In a series of decisions, the Court has said that, although Congress may induce states and municipalities to participate in federal programs by dangling federal funds in front of them, it may not actually "commandeer" state policymakers to do its bidding. Commandeering the states, the Court has said, interferes with the relationship between state policymaking officials and their constituents by diminishing the states' capacity to be responsible and accountable to their electorates. Without this capacity, the independent authority of the states would wither and these governments would become administrative appendages of Congress. It is not yet clear how far this new theory of the Tenth Amendment extends. The Brady Bill, by requiring that sheriffs implement a congressional handgun control program, has been challenged on exactly these grounds.

Although the effectiveness of statutory federalism depends on congressional self-restraint, constitutional federalism is, in principle, policed by the Court and thus potentially provides a more secure basis for state autonomy—as it did before the New Deal. Whether this is so in practice depends on the willingness and capacity of the Court to enforce these new boundaries. For example, if the Court were to find that the Brady Bill's commandeering sheriffs is unconstitutional, Congress can use its spending powers to achieve the same purpose. A similar conclusion holds for *Lopez*; it is not clear whether the congressional authority to regulate guns near schools would be struck down if Congress could provide a plausible link to interstate commerce, which it failed to do in the Gun Free School Zones Act.

Although people on both ends of the political spectrum bemoaned or celebrated *Lopez's* New Deal–shattering implications, whether it has such large implications depends on how it is elaborated both in subsequent decisions and in congressional explorations of the new constitutional terrain. A reinvigorated constitutional federalism might be attractive on the grounds that it would more securely reestablish the authority and responsibility of the states, but it is by no means clear how far the Court will go. Thus, statutory federalism, for all its political fragility, might be the only game in town, at least for now.

Several reasons suggest that redefining American federalism by statute is a good thing. For one, statutory federalism does not put the Supreme Court on a collision course with Congress. Historically, the Court has never been able to resist congressional assertions of authority for long, as the lessons of the New Deal demonstrate. Second, judicially imposed restraints are blunt tools in circumscribing congressional authority. As already suggested, the Brady Bill might have escaped constitutional scrutiny altogether had it relied on the spending clause instead of commandeering state officials. Its constitutionality has nothing to do with its substance or purposes, depending only on the specific legal forms through which these purposes were pursued. Third, refashioning commerce clause jurisprudence is a double-edged sword; narrowing the definition of commerce may limit congressional authority but at the price of limiting the authority of courts to restrain states from imposing interstate commercial barriers. Finally, statutory federalism places the policy question of which level of government is appropriate where it belongs: at the center of policy analysis and discussion and thus at the center of political debate. Statutory federalism does not presume that a particular program must be done at one level for constitutional reasons. Rather, the appropriate allocation of governmental tasks depends on the characteristics of the issues. Over time, because of technical or demographic changes, programs might properly be moved from one level to another without triggering constitutional questions.

Many leaders of both parties agree that, for many of our public problems, the states and localities should play a larger and more vigorous role than has been allowed to them in the past. The disagreements center on which problems to turn back to the states and how far the states may be trusted to address them. This volume is part of an effort to help resolve some of these disagreements by focusing on the issue of the "race to the bottom"—the standard objection to enlarging the role of states and localities. Often such arguments are raised in journalistic or political settings, where careful analysis is scarce.

Each contributor has taken seriously the possibility that interjurisdictional competition might have various adverse effects, but none finds much systematic evidence of a race to the bottom. Working in the welfare domain, an area where race-to-the-bottom arguments are common, Craig Volden shows that adverse effects of state competition are weak. Richard Revesz shows, in the area of environmental policy, the arguments for a race to the bottom are also weak, except when the specific policy concerns interjurisdictional spillovers. Moreover, he shows that federal attempts to alleviate the negative effects of interjurisdictional spillovers can be counterproductive. Roberta Romano shows that state competition for corporate charters has had generally beneficial effects on the structure of corporate law. This competition has permitted the emergence of one state, Delaware, leading the way in innovative law governing charters. The result has been a legal regime favorable to corporate governance and economic efficiency. Taken together, these essays undercut the idea that we ought, automatically, to be suspicious of programs in which states and localities play a substantial role.

A Look Ahead

Any analysis of federalism must resolve two political issues. First, as a matter of policy, the analysis must identify those problems best addressed at the state or local level and those best addressed at the national level. Second, the analysis must address the nature of states and localities as political units within the federal system. Although these political issues appear independent, they are not. If the states take on more responsibilities, they will become more vigorous and vital political units; they will therefore increasingly attract public attention and support, along with high-quality officials. In the early days of American federalism, politicians commonly left national offices to serve in their states. If states once again become "where the action is," their quality as political systems will improve.

Ironically, for the states to play the enhanced role the contributors envision for them successfully, they must also be limited in some ways. McKinnon and Nechyba argue that, for state competition to be beneficial, states must operate with hard budget constraints and be restrained (by the courts) from interfering with interstate commerce or shifting the costs of their policies to others. They show that the success of American federalism, relative to federalism in other countries, is partly traceable to two features: American states operate in the bond market's unforgiving, tight financial environment, and courts have prevented them from restraining interstate commerce. Thus, the new federalism, whether statutory or constitutional, retains a substantial role for national institutions. Nonetheless, McKinnon and Nechyba caution that federal attempts to deal with financial problems that fall within the states' domain have usually made thing worse.

For states and localities to address a wider range of policies effectively, they must be allowed to experiment with various approaches and to attract financial and other resources to meet their new responsibilities. The central issue of the new statutory federalism, therefore, is congressional restraint. But whether Congress can refrain from interfering in state domains is a difficult political issue. The movement toward new federalist solutions requires sustained popular support, which means that the people must stop expecting federal action on every problem. For the new federalism to be viable, congressional majorities must find the idea of restraint politically attractive. In the long run, this depends on the new federalism attracting sustained popular support in elections at all levels of the federal system.

CONTRIBUTORS

JOHN A. FEREJOHN is a senior fellow at the Hoover Institution and Carolyn S. G. Munro Professor of Political Science, Stanford University.

RONALD I. MCKINNON is Eberle Professor of Economics, Stanford University.

THOMAS J. NECHYBA is assistant professor of economics, Stanford University.

RICHARD L. REVESZ is professor of law at the New York University School of Law.

ROBERTA ROMANO is Allen Duffy/Class of 1960 Professor of Law, Yale Law School, Yale University.

CRAIG VOLDEN is visiting lecturer of Politics and Policy at the Irving B. Harris Graduate School of Public Policy Studies, University of Chicago.

BARRY R. WEINGAST is a senior fellow at the Hoover Institution and Ward C. Krebs Family Professor and chair of the Department of Political Science, Stanford University.

INDEX